Praise for *The Dangerous Book for Boys*

'The perfect handbook for boys and dads.'
Daily Telegraph

'Full of tips on how to annoy your parents.'
Evening Standard

'An old-fashioned compendium of information on items such as making catapults and knot-tyingthe end of the PlayStation may have been signalled.'   *The Times*

'Just William would be proud. A new book teaching boys old-fashioned risky pursuits...has become a surprise bestseller.'   *Daily Mail*

'If you want to know how to make crystals, master NATO's phonetic alphabet and build a workbench, look no further.'
Time Out

THE POCKET DANGEROUS BOOK FOR BOYS:

THINGS TO KNOW

Many of the pieces in this edition have been selected from the much-loved *The Dangerous Book for Boys*. They are a collection of useful trivia and information; things that every boy should know.

This edition is a perfect pocket format for readers to take everywhere with them. It has new drawings and new chapters full of fascinating facts.

The Pocket DANGEROUS Book for Boys

THINGS TO KNOW

Conn Iggulden & Hal Iggulden

HarperCollins*Publishers*

HarperCollins*Publishers*
77–85 Fulham Palace Road,
Hammersmith, London W6 8JB

www.harpercollins.co.uk

Published by HarperCollins*Publishers* 2008
1

A catalogue record for this book
is available from the British Library

ISBN-13: 978 0-00-725401-9

Set in Centennial by Andrew Ashton

Printed and bound in Italy by L.E.G.O. SpA – Vicenza

To all of those people who said 'You have to include...' until we had to avoid telling anyone else about the book for fear of the extra chapters. Particular thanks to Bernard Cornwell, whose advice helped us through a difficult time and Paul D'Urso, a good father and a good friend.

CONTENTS

INTRODUCTION

There's something magical about small books. Somehow you *own* them more than large ones. You can keep them in a secret box, or the crook of a tree. You can fit them into a coat pocket, or a rucksack. The original *Dangerous Book for Boys* couldn't have been made any smaller; we wanted to fit *everything* into it. The only problem was that it wasn't that portable which is a shame when you want it to be taken outside every now and then. What we've done here is conjured three pocket versions out of the book: *Things to Do*, *Things to Know* and *The Natural World**. We've added extra chapters too – you're going to love The Single Greatest Race of All Time – but if you're holding this, you'll know it's just the right size to take with you on adventures. The only thing we couldn't do was make it fireproof and waterproof, but who knows? Maybe we will, yet.

Conn Iggulden and Hal Iggulden

* Coming later

ANTHEMS

At a football or rugby game, it is really annoying when the crowd starts to sing and you can't join in because you don't know the words. To save you from this embarrassment, here are some of the most important anthems in Britain. If you take the time to learn them, they will give you immense pleasure in the years to come.

RULE BRITANNIA

Originally a poem by James Johnson (1700–1748), it was put to music by Thomas Augustine Arne in 1740. It is almost a second British national anthem.

When Britain first at Heav'n's command
Arose from out the azure main;
This was the charter of the land,
And guardian angels sang this strain:

Rule, Britannia! Britannia, rule the waves:
Britons never shall be slaves [Repeat].

The nations not so blest as thee,
Shall in their turns to tyrants fall;
While thou shalt flourish great and free,
The dread and envy of them all.

Rule Britannia etc...

Still more majestic shalt thou rise,
More dreadful from each foreign stroke;
As the loud blast that tears the skies,
Serves but to root thy native oak.

Rule Britannia etc...

Thee haughty tyrants ne'er shall tame,
All their attempts to bend thee down
Will but arouse thy generous flame;
But work their woe, and thy renown.

Rule Britannia etc...

To thee belongs the rural reign;
Thy cities shall with commerce shine;
All thine shall be the subject main,
And every shore it circles thine.

Rule Britannia etc...

The Muses, still with freedom found,
Shall to thy happy coast repair;
O blest Isle! With matchless beauty crowned,
And manly hearts to guide the fair.

Rule Britannia etc...

Note that the original lyrics had only one 'never' in the chorus, but it is now common practice to sing three of them: 'Britons never, never *ne-ver* will be slaves.'

England does not have an official national anthem, as *God Save the Queen* applies to the whole of the United Kingdom. This is the unofficial one, and others include *Jerusalem* and *Swing Low Sweet Chariot*.

Dear Land of Hope, thy hope is crowned.
God make thee mightier yet!
On Sov'reign brows, beloved, renowned,
Once more thy crown is set.
Thine equal laws, by Freedom gained,
Have ruled thee well and long;
By Freedom gained, by Truth maintained,
Thine Empire shall be strong.

Land of Hope and Glory, mother of the Free,
How shall we extol thee, who are born of thee?
Wider still and wider shall thy bounds be set;
God, who made thee mighty, make thee mightier yet

Thy fame is ancient as the days,
As Ocean large and wide
A pride that dares, and heeds not praise,
A stern and silent pride:
Not that false joy that dreams content
With what our sires have won;
The blood a hero sire hath spent
Still nerves a hero son.

Music by Elgar, words by A.C. Benson.

Scotland also has no official anthem beyond *God Save the Queen*, but it does have two unoffical ones in *Flower of Scotland* and the much older *Scotland the Brave*.

FLOWER OF SCOTLAND

O Flower of Scotland,
When will we see
your like again
That fought and died for
Your wee bit hill and glen.
And stood against him,
Proud Edward's army,
And sent him homeward
Tae think again.

The hills are bare now,
And autumn leaves
lie thick and still
O'er land that is lost now,
      Which those so dearly held
That stood against him,
Proud Edward's army
And sent him homeward
Tae think again.
Those days are past now
And in the past
they must remain

But we can still rise now
And be the nation again!
That stood against him
Proud Edward's army
And sent him homeward
Tae think again.

O Flower of Scotland,
When will we see
your like again
That fought and died for
Your wee bit hill and glen.
And stood against him,
Proud Edward's army,
And sent him homeward
Tae think again.

The 'proud Edward' above is Edward II of England, who fought and lost the battle of Bannockburn against the Scots in 1314. It was written by the Scottish folk singer Roy Williamson in 1966.

Wales is a principality – a state ruled by a prince. Like Scotland and England, it has unofficial anthems in *Land of Our Fathers*, *All Through the Night* and the wonderfully stirring *Men of Harlech*.

In Wales, *Land of Our Fathers* is usually sung in Welsh. In translation, the title is *Hen Wlad fy Nhadau*. The Welsh lyrics were written by Evan James in 1856, the tune composed by his son.

LAND OF OUR FATHERS

The land of my fathers, the land of my choice,
The land in which poets and minstrels rejoice;
The land whose stern warriors were true to the core,
While bleeding for freedom of yore.

Wales! Wales! fav'rite land of Wales!
While sea her wall, may naught befall
To mar the old language of Wales.

Old mountainous Cambria, the Eden of bards,
Each hill and each valley excite my regards;
To the ears of her patriots how charming still seems
The music that flows in her streams.

Wales! Wales etc...

My country tho' crushed by a hostile array,
The language of Cambria lives on to this day;
The muse has eluded the traitors' foul knives,
The harp of my country survives.

Wales! Wales etc...

Northern Ireland also has an unofficial anthem sung at the Commonwealth games. This beautiful tune is known as *The Londonderry Air*, composer unknown. There are various lyrics, but the most famous version is *Danny Boy*, written by Frederick Weatherly in 1913.

THE LONDONDERRY AIR

Oh Danny Boy, the pipes, the pipes are calling
From glen to glen, and down the mountain side
The summer's gone, and all the roses falling
'Tis you, 'tis you must go and I must bide
But come ye back when summer's in the meadow
Or when the valley's hushed and white with snow
'Tis I'll be here in sunshine or in shadow
Danny Boy, oh Danny Boy, I love you so
And when ye come, and all the flowers are dying
And I am dead, as dead I well may be
Ye'll come and find the place where I am lying
And kneel and say an Ave there for me
And I shall hear, though soft you tread above me
And all my grave shall warmer, sweeter be
For you shall bend and tell me that you love me
And I shall sleep in peace until you come to me.

Finally, the anthem of the United Kingdom, still used in New Zealand, Canada, Australia and the Commonwealth.

If the monarch is female, it's sung as *God Save the Queen*.
If male, it's *God Save the King*. In America, the same melody
is used for their patriotic song beginning 'My country, 'tis of
thee.' The origin of the tune is not known with any certainty.
The lyrics are sometimes attributed to Henry Carey.

GOD SAVE THE QUEEN

God save our gracious Queen,
Long live our noble Queen,
God save the Queen:
Send her victorious,
Happy and glorious,
Long to reign over us:
God save the Queen.

O Lord, our God, arise,
Scatter her enemies,
And make them fall.
Confound their politics,
Frustrate their knavish tricks,
On Thee our hopes we fix,
God save us all.

Thy choicest gifts in store,
On her be pleased to pour;
Long may she reign:
May she defend our laws,
And ever give us cause

To sing with heart and voice
God save the Queen.

Not in this land alone,
But be God's mercies known,
From shore to shore!
Lord make the nations see,
That men should brothers be,
And form one family,
The wide world o'er.

From every latent foe,
From the assassins blow,
God save the Queen!
O'er her thine arm extend,
For Britain's sake defend,
Our mother, prince, and friend,
God save the Queen!

Lord grant that Marshal Wade
May by thy mighty aid
Victory bring.
May he sedition hush,
And like a torrent rush,
Rebellious Scots to crush.
God save the Queen!

The final verse refers to the English army sent to crush the second Jacobite rebellion in 1745. As a result, the song is not that popular in Scotland. There are two more verses written later, but these are the original six.

EXTRAORDINARY STORIES –
PART ONE

———✦———

STORIES OF COURAGE and determination are sometimes underrated for their ability to inspire. It is true that once-famous names can slip from the memory of generations, names like Charles George Gordon, Richard Francis Burton, Florence Nightingale, Robert Scott, Herbert Kitchener, Henry Morton Stanley, Rudyard Kipling, Isambard Kingdom Brunel and a host of others. Their lives, their stories, were once known to every schoolboy; held up as examples of fortitude and honour. These values have not ceased to be important in the modern world, nor have the stories become less moving. We have chosen five of our favourites. They range from Nelson's death at Trafalgar to the astonishing modern story of Joe Simpson's struggle in the mountains of Peru. These are all tales worth knowing.

Robert Scott and the Antarctic

Robert Falcon Scott was born on 6 June 1868. All his life, he was known as 'Con', a short form of his middle name. He came from a seafaring family, with uncles, grand-uncles and grandparents all serving in the Royal Navy. His father owned a small brewery in Plymouth that had been bought with prize money from the Napoleonic wars.

'Con' Scott joined HMS *Boadicea* at the age of thirteen

as a midshipman. It was a hard world, requiring instant obedience and personal discipline. By twenty-two, he was a lieutenant with first-class certificates in pilotage (steering/navigation), torpedoes and gunnery, with the highest marks in his year for seamanship.

He had met Sir Clements Markham, the President of the Royal Geographical Society, more than once in the course of his naval duties, impressing the older man with his intelligence and demeanour. When, at the turn of the century, the Royal Society wanted someone to head an expedition to the South Pole, Sir Clements Markham fought to have Scott lead the group.

Scott had no experience of the extremes he would be facing at that point in his career. He solved this problem by consulting those who had, travelling to Oslo to consult Fridtjof Nansen, a Norwegian explorer of Arctic regions who would later become the Norwegian ambassador to London. They became firm friends and Scott accepted Nansen's advice to get dogs to pull sleds, buying twenty dogs and three bitches in Russia for his first attempt on the South Pole.

By 1900, the first members of the team were appointed. Scott had insisted on personal approval of all appointments and was able to make quick decisions. With an idea of the hardship ahead, most were young and fit, though when Scott met Edward Wilson, a young doctor and artist, the man was suffering from an abscess in his armpit, blood poisoning and lungs weakened by tuberculosis. Nonetheless, Scott appointed him. He also chose one

Robert Scott

Ernest Shackleton, whose own courageous story would become famous later on.

With the money Sir Clements Markham had raised, the ship *Discovery* was built, costing £49,277, and launched on 21 March 1901. Scott also purchased a balloon for the voyage, costing £1300. The young King and Queen, Edward VII and Alexandra, came on board to see the ship at Cowes. Sir Clements Markham said of the crew, 'No finer set of men ever left these shores, nor were men ever led by a finer captain.'

The trip south was slow and difficult. *Discovery* leaked and could not make more than seven knots under full steam. However, they reached New Zealand and had the leak fixed as well as taking on supplies. They sailed on into the ice packs and the high southern latitudes. Scott and Shackleton were the first people ever to take a balloon trip in the Antarctic, though that too developed a leak and was used only once.

Their lack of experience showed in a number of ways, from misjudging distances and the difficulties of driving dogs, to protecting the skin and cooking in low temperatures. They had to learn vital skills very quickly in an environment where sweat froze and a blizzard could strike without warning. However, they did learn, spending a year in an icy landscape, out of which their ship seemed to grow.

In November 1902, they made a push to the Pole, but the dogs sickened. They were the first to cross the 80th parallel, after which all maps were blank. They began to kill the dogs, feeding them to the others. Shackleton developed the first symptoms of scurvy due to a lack of vitamins in his diet and the pain of snow blindness became so great for Wilson that he had to use a blindfold and follow Scott's voice. After an attempt lasting ninety-three days, they were four hundred and eighty miles from the Pole when Scott gave the order to turn back on 31 December. More dogs died on the way back to the ship, but the men all survived to try again.

A support ship, the *Morning*, resupplied the expedition and took some members home, including Shackleton. Research trips continued, despite recording temperatures as low as –67°F. The *Discovery* had become solidly wedged and it took a combination of relief ships and dynamite to free her after two years on the ice. They returned to Portsmouth in September 1904. Still on special leave from the Royal Navy, Scott was appointed Captain on the strength of his achievements. There were exhibitions of drawings and scientific samples, lectures and tours. Scott became something of a celebrity, publishing a two-volume account of the expedition, complete with Wilson's dramatic pictures. Despite his relative success, the government ignored Scott's plea to save the *Discovery* and she was sold.

In 1907, Scott went back to sea as Captain on various ships, and met and married Kathleen Bruce in 1908. Shackleton tried a trip of his own, but his team turned back when they were only ninety-seven miles from the Pole. The lure of the Antarctic had struck deep in both Scott and Shackleton, but it was Scott's second expedition of 1910 that was to become famous around the world.

Scott wrote that 'the main object of the expedition is to reach the South Pole and secure for the British Empire the honour of that achievement.' Science would play a lesser part in the second strike for the Pole.

Scott had learned from his previous experiences and consulted once again with Nansen while the money was raised and the team came together. Funds came slowly and more than one member of the expedition collected money to earn their place. Captain L.E.G. Oates was in charge of ponies. Wilfred Bruce, Scott's brother-in-law, was sent to Russia to buy the vital sled-dogs and Siberian ponies. They also experimented with motor sledges.

The Norwegian explorer Roald Amundsen was also heading south. Originally, his intentions had been to explore the Arctic, but an American, Robert Peary, claimed to have reached the North Pole in 1909 and Amundsen now had his sights set on the unconquered southern pole. He had a hundred dogs with him and supplies for two years. He knew the conditions and he had planned the route. Scott was still struggling to collect funds in New Zealand and Australia. The final stores were loaded and the ship *Terra Nova* sailed on 29 November 1910. Two months before, Scott had received a telegram from Amundsen, sent after he had sailed. It had read only, 'Beg leave inform you proceeding Antarctic. Amundsen.'

Terra Nova entered the pack ice on 9 December, smashing its way through and finally anchoring to solid ice in January 1911. The sledges, base equipment and supplies were unloaded – and the heaviest motor sledge broke through the ice, disappearing into the sea. The slow process of a pole attempt began, with camps established further and further south. The ponies did not do at all well and frostbite appeared very early on amongst the men.

Captain L.E.G. Oates

Conditions were awful, with constant blizzards pinning them in their tents. The ponies were all dead by the time they reached the last camp, after dragging the sledges up a 10,000-foot glacier. Scott picked Wilson, Evans, Oates and Bowers for the final slog to the Pole, with each man hauling 200 pounds on sledges.

The smaller team of five battled through blizzards to reach the 89th parallel, the last before the Pole itself. It was shortly afterwards that they crossed the tracks of Amundsen and his dog teams. Scott and the others were touched by despair, but went on regardless, determined to reach the Pole.

They finally stood at the southernmost point on earth on 17 January 1912. There they found a tent, with a piece of paper that bore the names of five men: Roald Amundsen, Olav Olavson Bjaaland, Sverre Hassel, Oscar Wisting and Hilmer Hanssen. The note was dated 14 December 1911. The disappointment weighed heavily on all of them – there have been few closer races in history with so much at stake.

The return journey began well enough, but Evans had lost fingernails to the cold, Wilson had strained a tendon in his leg, Scott himself had a bruised shoulder and Oates had the beginnings of gangrene in his toes. In such extreme conditions of exhaustion, even small wounds refused to heal. They had all paid a terrible price to be second.

Food began to run short and every supply dump they reached was a race against starvation and the cold. Oil too ran low and freezing to death was a real possibility. Evans collapsed on 16 February and never fully recovered. He struggled on the following day, but he could barely stand and died shortly afterwards.

Wilson too was growing weak, so Scott and Bowers made camp by themselves in temperatures of –43 °F.

On 16 or 17 March, Oates said he could not go on and wanted to be left in his sleeping bag. He knew he was slowing them down, and that their only slim chance may have been vanishing. The next morning, there was a blizzard blowing. Oates stood up in the tent and said, 'I am just going outside and may be some time.'

Scott wrote in his diary, 'We knew that poor Oates was walking to his death, but though we tried to dissuade him, we knew it was the act of a brave man and an English gentleman.' Oates was not seen again and his body has never been found.

By 20 March, Scott knew he would lose his right foot to frostbite. They were only eleven miles from a camp, but a blizzard prevented them from moving on and staying still was a slow death for the three men remaining. They had run out of oil and had only two days of starvation rations left. They had run out of time and strength. Scott made the decision to try for the depot, but it was beyond them and they did not leave that last position. Scott's final diary entry was, 'It seems a pity, but I do not think that I can write more. R. Scott. For God's sake look after our people.'

With the diary ended, Scott wrote letters to the families of those who had died, including a letter to his own wife, where he mentioned their only son.

I had looked forward to helping you to bring him up, but it is a satisfaction to know that he will be safe with you...

Make the boy interested in natural history if you can. It is better than games. They encourage it in some schools. I know you will keep him in the open air. Try to make him believe in a God, it is comforting... and guard him against indolence. Make him a strenuous man. I had to force myself into being strenuous, as you know – had always an inclination to be idle.

He also wrote a letter to the public, knowing that his body would be found.

We took risks, we knew we took them; things have come out against us, and therefore we have no cause for complaint, but bow to the will of providence, determined still to do our best to the last... Had we lived, I should have had a tale to tell of the hardihood, endurance and courage of my companions which would have stirred the heart of every Englishman. These rough notes and our dead bodies must tell the tale, but surely, surely, a great rich country like ours will see that those who are dependent on us are properly provided for.

Scott knew that the expedition funds were crippled by debt and his last thoughts were the fear that their loved ones would be made destitute by what was still owed. In fact, enough donations came in when the story was known to pay all debts and create grants for the children and wives of those who had perished.

The men were found frozen in their tent by the team surgeon, Atkinson, in November of that year. The diaries and letters were recovered, but a snow cairn was built over their last resting place ready for the day when the moving pack ice would ease them into the frozen sea. The search party looked for Oates without success, finally erecting a cross to him with the following inscription.

HEREABOUTS DIED A VERY GALLANT
GENTLEMAN, Captain L.E.G. Oates OF THE
INNISKILLING DRAGOONS. IN MARCH 1912,
RETURNING FROM THE POLE, HE WALKED
WILLINGLY TO HIS DEATH IN A BLIZZARD
TO TRY TO SAVE HIS COMRADES, BESET
BY HARDSHIP.

'. . . for my own sake I do not regret this journey, which has shown that Englishmen can endure hardships, help one another, and meet death with as great a fortitude as ever in the past.'
— Robert Falcon Scott

THE DAILY MIRROR, Wednesday, May 21, 1913.

CAPTAIN SCOTT'S TOMB NEAR THE SOUTH POLE.

The Daily Mirror

24 Pages

THE MORNING JOURNAL WITH THE SECOND LARGEST NET SALE.

No. 2,987. Registered at the G.P.O. as a Newspaper. WEDNESDAY, MAY 21, 1913 One Halfpenny.

 THE MOST WONDERFUL MONUMENT IN THE WORLD: CAPTAIN SCOTT'S SEPULCHRE ERECTED AMID ANTARCTIC WASTES.

It was within a mere eleven miles of One Ton camp, which would have meant safety to the Antarctic explorers, that the search party found the tent containing the bodies of Captain Scott, Dr. E. A. Wilson and Lieutenant H. R. Bowers. This is, perhaps, the most tragic note of the whole Antarctic disaster. Above is the cairn, surmounted with a cross, erected over the tent where the bodies were found. At the side are Captain Scott's skis planted upright in a small pile of frozen snow.—(Copyright in England. Droits de reproduction en France réservés.)

EXTRAORDINARY STORIES – PART ONE

THE TWELVE TABLES
OF ROMAN LAW

ONE OF THE REASONS we look back so fondly on ancient Rome is that the culture was a beacon of civilisation at a time in history where places like Britain were still dark, savage and tribal. As early as the fifth century BC, laws were inscribed or painted onto twelve wooden tablets. The first ten were written by Patricians, the ruling class; the final two were produced by Patricians and Plebeians, the common men of Rome. Later they were 'set in stone' and achieved a revered status very similar to the modern American Constitution. When Cicero was young, school-boys were expected to memorise them as a matter of course.

In later centuries, the core of laws was amended, inter-preted and occasionally challenged by public law cases. Though the Roman writer Livy described them as 'the fountain of all public and private law', they would run alongside a greater body of more complex common law created from cases. Julius Caesar was a public defender, as was Brutus, his assassin. The greatest Roman orator, Cicero was no supporter of Caesar, but even he was impressed by the man's rhetoric and public debate. As well as martial skill, a rising young lion of Rome was expected to be able to speak well and have a grounding in the laws of the Roman state.

By the time Justinian became emperor of the Eastern Roman Empire in 527AD, the body of laws had become unwieldy and unnecessarily complex. With the help of the best legal minds of the day, Justinian rewrote the entire code in a form that would later become the foundation of modern law.

In the period of the British Empire, many laws had their origin in the Roman system. The customary laws of the Channel Islands, the law of Scotland and the Roman-Dutch law in South Africa and Ceylon all relate back to the statutes and practices of Rome.

It is an impressive legacy. Sadly, the original text survives only in fragments and references, though we have enough to produce the text below. The laws themselves were often brutal by modern standards and make fascinating reading.

THE TWELVE TABLES OF ROMAN LAW

Though all the world exclaim against me, I will say what I think: that single little book of the Twelve Tables, if anyone look to the fountains and sources of laws, seems to me, assuredly, to surpass the libraries of all the philosophers, both in weight of authority, and in plenitude of utility. Cicero, *De Oratore*

TABLE I

1. If anyone summons a man before the magistrate, he must go. If the man summoned does not go, let the one summoning him call the bystanders to witness and then take him by force.
2. If he shirks or runs away, let the summoner lay hands on him.
3. If illness or old age is the hindrance, let the summoner provide a team. He need not provide a covered carriage with a pallet unless he chooses.
4. Let the protector of a landholder be a landholder; for one of the proletariat, let anyone that cares, be protector.

6-9. When the litigants settle their case by compromise, let the magistrate announce it. If they do not compromise, let them state each his own side of the case, in the *comitium* of the forum before noon. Afterwards let them talk it out together, while both are present. After noon, in case either party has failed to appear, let the magistrate pronounce judgment in favor of the one who is present. If both are present the trial may last until sunset but no later.

TABLE II

2. He whose witness has failed to appear may summon
   him by loud calls before his house every third day.

TABLE III

1. One who has confessed a debt, or against whom judgment has been pronounced, shall have thirty days to
   pay. After that forcible seizure of his person is allowed.
   The creditor shall bring him before the magistrate.
   Unless he pays the amount of the judgment or someone
   in the presence of the magistrate interferes in his behalf
   as protector, the creditor shall take him home and fasten him in stocks or fetters. He shall fasten him with not
   less than fifteen pounds of weight or, if he choose, with
   more. If the prisoner choose, he may furnish his own
   food. If he does not, the creditor must give him a pound
   of meal daily; if he choose he may give him more.
2. On the third market day, let them divide his body
   among them. If they cut more or less than each one's
   share it shall be no crime.
3. Against a foreigner the right in property shall be valid
   forever.

TABLE IV

1. A dreadfully deformed child shall be quickly killed.
2. If a father sell his son three times, the son shall be free
   from his father.

3. As a man has provided in his will in regard to his money and the care of his property, so let it be binding. If he has no heir and dies intestate, let the nearest agnate (relation by blood on his father's side) have the inheritance. If there is no agnate, let the members of his gens (family or tribe) have the inheritance.
4. If one is mad but has no guardian, the power over him and his money shall belong to his agnates and the members of his *gens*.
5. A child born after ten months since the father's death will not be admitted into a legal inheritance.

TABLE V

1. Females should remain in guardianship even when they have attained their majority.

TABLE VI

1. When one makes a bond and a conveyance of property, as he has made formal declaration, so let it be binding.
3. A beam that is built into a house or a vineyard trellis one may not take from its place.
5. *Usucapio* (ownership) of movable things requires one year's possession for its completion; but *usucapio* of an estate and buildings two years.
6. Any woman who does not wish to be subjected in this manner to the hand of her husband should be absent three nights in succession every year, and so interrupt the *usucapio* of each year.

TABLE VII

1. Let them keep the road in order. If they have not paved it, a man may drive his team where he likes.
9. Should a tree on a neighbour's farm be bent crooked by the wind and lean over your farm, you may take legal action for removal of that tree.
10. A man might gather up fruit that was falling down onto another man's farm.

TABLE VIII

2. If one has maimed a limb and does not compromise with the injured person, let there be retaliation. If one has broken a bone of a freeman with his hand or with a stick, let him pay a penalty of three hundred coins. If he has broken the bone of a slave, let him have one hundred and fifty coins. If one is guilty of insult, the penalty shall be twenty-five coins.
3. If one is slain while committing theft by night, he is rightly slain.
4. If a patron shall have devised any deceit against his client, let him be accursed.
5. If one shall permit himself to be summoned as a witness, but does not give his testimony, let him be noted as dishonest and incapable of acting again as witness.
10. Any person who destroys by burning any building or heap of corn deposited alongside a house shall be bound, scourged, and put to death by burning at the

stake provided that he has committed the said misdeed with malice aforethought; but if he shall have committed it by accident, that is, by negligence, he must repair the damage. If he be too poor for such punishment, he shall receive a lighter punishment.

12. If the theft has been done by night, if the owner kills the thief, the thief shall be held to be lawfully killed.

13. It is unlawful for a thief to be killed by day unless he defends himself with a weapon. Even though he has come with a weapon, unless he shall use the weapon and fight back, you shall not kill him. And even if he resists, first call out so that someone may hear and come up.

23. A person who had been found guilty of giving false witness shall be hurled down from the Tarpeian Rock.

26. No person shall hold meetings by night in the city.

TABLE IX

4. The penalty shall be capital for a judge or arbiter legally appointed who has been found guilty of receiving a bribe for giving a decision.

5. Treason: he who shall have roused up a public enemy or handed over a citizen to a public enemy must suffer capital punishment.

6. Putting to death of any man, whosoever he might be unconvicted is forbidden.

TABLE X

1. None is to bury or burn a corpse in the city.
3. The women shall not tear their faces nor wail on account of the funeral.
5. If one obtains a crown himself, or if his chattel does so because of his honour and valour, if it is placed on his head, or the head of his parents, it shall be no crime.

TABLE XI

1. Marriages should not take place between plebeians and patricians.

TABLE XII

2. If a slave shall have committed theft or done damage with his master's knowledge, the action for damages is in the slave's name.
5. Whatever the people had last ordained should be held as binding by law.

SPIES – CODES AND CIPHERS

⟨✳⟩

Tʜᴇ ᴘʀᴀᴄᴛɪᴄᴇ ᴏғ ꜱᴇɴᴅɪɴɢ secret messages is known as 'steganography', Greek for 'concealed writing'. The problem with hiding a message in the lining of a coat or tattooed on the scalp is that anyone can read it. It makes a lot of sense to practise 'cryptography', as well, Greek for 'hidden writing'. Cryptography is the art of writing or breaking codes and ciphers.

The words 'code' and 'cipher' are sometimes used as if they mean the same thing. They do not. A code is a substitution, such as the following sentence: 'The Big Cheese lands at Happy tomorrow.' We do not know who the 'Big Cheese' is, or where 'Happy' is. Codes were commonly used between spies in World War II, when groups of numbers could only be translated with the correct codebook. Codes are impossible to break without a key or detailed knowledge of the people involved. If you spied on a group for some months, however, noticing the President of France landed at Heathrow airport the day after such a message, a pattern might begin to emerge.

'Ciphers', on the other hand, are scrambled messages, not a secret language. In a cipher, a plain-text message is concealed by replacing the letters according to a pattern. Even Morse Code is, in fact, a cipher. They are fascinating and even dangerous. More than one person has gone to his grave without giving up the secret of a particular cipher. Treasures have been lost, along with lives spent searching for them. In time of war, thousands of lives can depend on ciphers being kept – or '*deciphered*'.

Edgar Allan Poe left behind a cipher that was only broken in the year 2000. The composer Elgar left a message for a young lady that has not yet been fully understood. Treasure codes exist that point the way to huge sums in gold – if only the sequence of symbols can be broken.

At the time of writing, the state-of-the-art cipher is a computer sequence with 2048 figures, each of which can be a number, letter or symbol. The combinations are in trillions of trillions and it is estimated that even the fastest computers in the world couldn't break it in less than thirty billion years. Oddly enough, it was created by a seventeen-year-old boy in Kent, named Peter Parkinson. He is quite pleased with it. To put it in perspective, it is illegal in America to export an encryption program with more than *forty* digits without providing a key. It takes three days to break a 56-bit encryption.

Combinations to computer locks are one thing. This chapter contains some classic ciphers – starting with the one used by Julius Caesar to send messages to his generals.

1. **The Caesar Shift Cipher.** This is a simple alphabet cipher – but tricky to break without the key. Each letter is moved along by a number – say four. A becomes E, J becomes N, Z becomes D and so on. The number is the key to the cipher here. Caesar could agree the number with his generals in private and then send encrypted

messages knowing they could not be read without that crucial extra piece of information.

'The dog is sick' becomes 'WKH GRJ LV VLFN', with the number three as the key.

As a first cipher it works well, but the problem is that there are only twenty-five possible number choices (twenty-six would take you back to the letter you started with). As a result, someone who really wanted to break the code could simply plod their way through all twenty-five combinations. Admittedly, they would first have to recognise the code as a Caesar cipher, but this one only gets one star for difficulty – it is more than two thousand years old, after all.

2. **Numbers.** A = 1, B = 2, C = 3 etc, all the way to Z = 26. Messages can be written using those numbers. This cipher is probably too simple to use on its own; however, if you combine it with a Caesar code number, it can suddenly become very tricky indeed.

In the basic method, 'The dog is better' would be '20 8 5 – 4 15 7 – 9 19 – 2 5 20 20 5 18', which looks difficult but isn't. Add a Caesar cipher of 3, however, and the message becomes '3 23 11 8 – 7 18 10 – 12 22 – 5 8 23 23 8 21', which should overheat the brain of younger brothers or sisters trying to break the encryption. Note that we have included the key number at the beginning. It could be agreed beforehand in private to make this even harder to break. (With the Caesar combination, a difficulty of two stars.)

3. **Alphabet ciphers.** There are any number of these. Most of them depend on the way the alphabet is written out – agreed beforehand between the spies.

A B C D E F G H I J K L M

N O P Q R S T U V W X Y Z

With this sequence, 'How are you?' would become 'UBJ NER LBH?'

A B C D E F G H I J K L M N O P Q R S T U V W X Y Z

Z Y X W V U T S R Q P O N M L K J I H G F E D C B A

In this one, 'How are you?' would become 'SLD ZIV BLF?' It's worth remembering that even simple ciphers are not obvious at first glance. Basic alphabet ciphers may be enough to protect a diary and they have the benefit of being easy to use and remember.

4. Most famous of the alphabet variations is a code stick – another one used by the Romans. Begin with a strip of paper and wind it around a stick. It is important that the sender and the receiver both have the same type. Two bits from the same broom handle would be perfect, but most people end up trying this on a pencil. (See picture.)

Here the word 'Heathrow' is written down the length of the pencil, with a couple of letters per turn of the strip. (You'll need to hold the paper steady with tape, or better still, Blu-Tack.) When the tape is unwound, the same pen is used to fill in the spaces between the letters. It should now look like gibberish. The idea is that when it is wound back on to a similar stick, the message will be clear. It is a cipher that requires a bit of forethought, but can be quite satisfying. For a matter of life and death, however, you may need the next method.

5. **Codeword alphabet substitution.** You might have noticed a pattern developing here. To make a decent cipher, it is a good idea to agree the key beforehand. It could be a number, a date, the title of a book, a word or even a kind of stick. It's the sort of added complexity that can make even a simple encryption quite fiendish.

Back to one of our earlier examples:

A B C D E F G H I J K L M N O P Q R S T U V W X Y Z

Z Y X W V U T S R Q P O N M L K J I H G F E D C B A

If we added the word 'WINDOW', we would get the sequence below. Note that no letters are repeated, so there are still twenty-six in the bottom sequence and the second 'W' of 'WINDOW' is not used.

A B C D E F G H I J K L M N O P Q R S T U V W X Y Z

W I N D O A B C E F G H J K L M P Q R S T U V X Y Z

This is a whole new cipher – and without knowing the codeword, a difficulty of three stars to crack.

6. **Cipher-wheels.** Using a pair of compasses, cut four circles out of card, two large and two small – 5 inch (12 cm) and 4 inch (10 cm) diameters work well. For both pairs, put one on top of the other and punch a hole through with a butterfly stud. They should rotate easily.

A circle = 360 degrees. There are twenty-six letters in the alphabet, so the spacing for the segments should be approximately 14 degrees. Mark off the segments as accurately as you can for all four circles. When they are ready, write the normal alphabet around the outside of the large circles in the usual way – A to Z. For the inner circles, mark the letters in random order. As long as the matching code wheel is done in the same way, it doesn't matter where the letters go. The code sequence will begin with the two-letter combination that shows the positions of the wheels – AM or AF, for example.

You should end up with a cipher-wheel encrypter that can *only* be read by someone with the other wheel. Now *that* is a difficulty of four stars.

7. **Morse Code** is the most famous substitution cipher ever invented. It was thought up by an American inventor, Samuel F.B. Morse, who patented a telegraph system and saw it explode in popularity. He realised that a pulse of electricity could act on an electromagnet to move a simple lever – transmitting a long or short signal. He arranged a moving strip of paper to pass underneath the metal point and a new method of communication was born. Using his cipher, he sent the first inter-city message in 1844 from Washington to Baltimore. The marvellous thing about it is that the code can be sent using light if you have a torch, or sound, if you can reach a car horn, or even semaphore, though that is fairly tricky.

The first message Morse sent was 'What hath God wrought?', which gives an idea of just how impressive it was to pick up messages as they were written on the other side of America. In Morse's lifetime, he saw telegraph lines laid across the Atlantic.

MORSE CODE

A •–	**N** –•	**1** •––––
B –•••	**O** –––	**2** ••–––
C –•–•	**P** •––•	**3** •••––
D –••	**Q** ––•–	**4** ••••–
E •	**R** •–•	**5** •••••
F ••–•	**S** •••	**6** –••••
G ––•	**T** –	**7** ––•••
H ••••	**U** ••–	**8** –––••
I ••	**V** •••–	**9** ––––•
J •–––	**W** •––	**0** –––––
K –•–	**X** –••–	
L •–••	**Y** –•––	
M ––	**Z** ––••	

The example *everyone* knows is SOS – the international distress call. ('May-day' is also well known. That one comes from the French for 'Help me' – 'M'aidez'.)

The SOS sequence in Morse is dit dit dit – dah dah dah – dit dit dit.

This really is one worth learning. Rescuers have heard messages tapped out underneath fallen buildings, heard whistles or seen the flashes from a capsized dinghy. This cipher has saved a large number of lives over the years since its invention. It has also sent quite a few train timetables.

If you *do* have a flag handy, it's left for a dash, right for a dot. This is not so well known.

8. This last one is actually designed to make meaning clearer rather than to hide it. The **Nato Phonetic alphabet** is just useful to know.

A previous RAF version (c.1924-1942) was Ace, Beer, Charlie, Don, Edward, Freddie, George, Harry, Ink, Johnnie, King, London, Monkey, Nuts, Orange, Pip, Queen, Robert, Sugar, Toc, Uncle, Vic, William, X-ray, Yorker, Zebra. This was more suited to British English accents, apparently. The Nato version was created in 1956 and has become the accepted standard phonetic alphabet. It is used to minimise confusion when reading letters aloud on the radio or telephone. 'P' and 'B' sound very similar – but 'Papa' and 'Bravo' do not.

NATO PHONETIC ALPHABET

A	Alpha	N	November
B	Bravo	O	Oscar
C	Charlie	P	Papa
D	Delta	Q	Quebec
E	Echo	R	Romeo
F	Foxtrot	S	Sierra
G	Golf	T	Tango
H	Hotel	U	Uniform
I	India	V	Victor
J	Juliet	W	Whiskey
K	Kilo	X	X-ray
L	Lima	Y	Yankee
M	Mike	Z	Zulu

FIVE POEMS EVERY BOY SHOULD KNOW

※

Yes, a boy should be able to climb trees, grow crystals and tie a decent bowline knot. However, a boy will grow into a man and no man should be completely ignorant of these poems. They are the ones that spoke to us when we were young. Find a big tree and climb it. Read one of these poems aloud to yourself, high in the branches. All the authors are long dead, but they may still speak to you.

IF –

BY RUDYARD KIPLING (1865–1936)

If you can keep your head when all about you
Are losing theirs and blaming it on you,
If you can trust yourself when all men doubt you,
But make allowance for their doubting too;
If you can wait and not be tired by waiting,
Or being lied about, don't deal in lies,
Or being hated, don't give way to hating,
And yet don't look too good, nor talk too wise:

If you can dream – and not make dreams your master;
If you can think – and not make thoughts your aim;

If you can meet with Triumph and Disaster
*   And treat those two impostors just the same;*
If you can bear to hear the truth you've spoken
*   Twisted by knaves to make a trap for fools,*
Or watch the things you gave your life to, broken,
*   And stoop and build 'em up with worn-out tools:*

If you can make one heap of all your winnings
*   And risk it on one turn of pitch-and-toss,*
And lose, and start again at your beginnings
*   And never breathe a word about your loss;*
If you can force your heart and nerve and sinew
*   To serve your turn long after they are gone,*
And so hold on when there is nothing in you
*   Except the Will which says to them: 'Hold on!'*

If you can talk with crowds and keep your virtue,
*   Or walk with Kings – nor lose the common touch,*
If neither foes nor loving friends can hurt you,
*   If all men count with you, but none too much;*
If you can fill the unforgiving minute
*   With sixty seconds' worth of distance run,*
Yours is the Earth and everything that's in it,
*   And – which is more – you'll be a Man, my son!*

We recommend *Puck of Pook's Hill* as an example of Kipling's prose. Tragically, his only son John was killed in the First World War, in 1915.

Ozymandias

BY PERCY BYSSHE SHELLEY (1792–1822)

I met a traveller from an antique land
Who said: Two vast and trunkless legs of stone
Stand in the desert ... Near them, on the sand,
Half sunk, a shattered visage lies, whose frown,
And wrinkled lip, and sneer of cold command,
Tell that its sculptor well those passions read
Which yet survive, stamped on these lifeless things,
The hand that mocked them, and the heart that fed:
And on the pedestal these words appear:
'My name is Ozymandias, king of kings:
Look on my works, ye Mighty, and despair!'
Nothing beside remains. Round the decay
Of that colossal wreck, boundless and bare
The lone and level sands stretch far away.

This poem was written as a commentary on human arrogance. It is based on a broken statue near Luxor, Egypt. The actual inscription (translated) reads 'King of Kings am I, Osymandias. If anyone would know how great I am and where I lie, let him surpass one of my works.'

Invictus

BY WILLIAM ERNEST HENLEY (1849–1903)

Out of the night that covers me,
*   Black as the pit from pole to pole,*
I thank whatever gods may be
*   For my unconquerable soul.*

In the fell clutch of circumstance
*   I have not winced nor cried aloud.*
Under the bludgeonings of chance
*   My head is bloody, but unbowed.*

Beyond this place of wrath and tears
*   Looms but the Horror of the shade,*
And yet the menace of the years
*   Finds, and shall find, me unafraid.*

It matters not how strait the gate,
*   How charged with punishments the scroll,*
I am the master of my fate:
*   I am the captain of my soul.*

'Invictus' is Latin for 'unconquerable'. As a child, Henley suffered the amputation of a foot. He was ill for much of his life and wrote this during a two-year spell in an infirmary. He was a great friend of Robert Louis Stevenson and the character of Long John Silver may even be based on him.

Vitae Lampada

SIR HENRY NEWBOLT (1862–1938)

There's a breathless hush in the Close tonight –
*   Ten to make and the match to win –*
A bumping pitch and a blinding light,
*   An hour to play and the last man in.*
And it's not for the sake of a ribboned coat,
*   Or the selfish hope of a season's fame,*
But his Captain's hand on his shoulder smote –
*   'Play up! play up! and play the game!'*

The sand of the desert is sodden red, –
*   Red with the wreck of a square that broke; –*
The Gatling's jammed and the Colonel dead,
*   And the regiment blind with dust and smoke.*
The river of death has brimmed his banks,
*   And England's far, and Honour a name,*
But the voice of a schoolboy rallies the ranks:
*   'Play up! play up! and play the game!'*

This is the word that year by year,
*   While in her place the School is set,*
Every one of her sons must hear,
*   And none that hears it dare forget.*
This they all with a joyful mind
*   Bear through life like a torch in flame,*
And falling fling to the host behind –
*   'Play up! play up! and play the game!'*

Though the poem makes reference to a British square of soldiers being broken in the Sudan, the poem is actually about the importance of passing on values to the generations after us. In the poem, the young soldier remembers his old Captain's words to rally his men. 'Vitaē Lampada' came out in 1898. It means 'the torch of life'.

Sea-Fever
BY JOHN MASEFIELD (1878–1967)

I must down to the seas again, to the lonely sea and the sky,
And all I ask is a tall ship and a star to steer her by,
And the wheel's kick and the wind's song and the white
*   sails shaking,*
And a grey mist on the sea's face and a grey dawn breaking.

I must down to the seas again, for the call of the running tide
Is a wild call and a clear call that may not be denied;
And all I ask is a windy day with the white clouds flying,
And the flung spray and the blown spume, and the sea-gulls
*   crying.*

I must down to the seas again, to the vagrant gypsy life,
To the gull's way and the whale's way where the wind's like
*   a whetted knife;*
And all I ask is a merry yarn from a laughing fellow-rover,
And quiet sleep and a sweet dream when the long trick's
*   over.*

Masefield, who later became Poet Laureate, wrote 'Sea-Fever' when he was only twenty-two. It contains some fantastic examples of onomatopoeia – words that sound like their meaning. You can hear the wind in 'wind like a whetted knife', for example.

There are hundreds more poems that have stayed with us as we grow older. That is the magic perhaps, that a single line can bring comfort in grief, or express the joy of a birth. These are not small things.

KINGS AND QUEENS OF ENGLAND AND SCOTLAND

House of Alpin (Scotland)

843–859	Kenneth Macalpin.
860–863	Donald I
864–877	Constantine I
877–878	Aed
878–889	Eochaid
889–900	Donald II
900–942	Constantine II

House of Dunkeld

942–954	Malcolm I
954–962	Indulf
962–967	Dubh
967–971	Cuilean
971–995	Kenneth II
995–997	Constantine III
997–1005	Kenneth III
1005–1034	Malcolm II
1034–1040	Duncan
1040–1057	Macbeth
1057–1058	Lulach 'The Fool'

The House of Canmore

1058–1093	Malcolm III
1093–1094	Donald Ban
May to November 1094	
	Duncan II
1094–1097	Donald Ban and Edmund
1097–1107	Edgar 'The Peaceable'
1107–1124	Alexander the Fierce
1124–1153	David I
1153–1165	Malcolm IV 'The Maiden'
1165–1214	William the Lion.
1214–1249	Alexander II
1249–1286	Alexander III
1286–1290	Margaret (Maid of Norway)

Disputed succession.

The House of Balliol

1292–1296   John Balliol.
             Resigned his
             Kingdom to
             Edward I of
             England. Died In
             Normandy.

The House of Bruce

1306–1329   Robert I (The
             Bruce)
1329–1371   David II

The House of Stewart

1371–1390   Robert II
1390–1406   Robert III
1406–1437   James I
1437–1460   James II
1460–1488   James III
1488–1513   James IV
1513–1542   James V
1542–1567   Mary Queen of
             Scots
1567–1603   James VI – who
             later became king
             of England in 1603
             when Elizabeth I
             died without heirs.

Royal Standard
of the King of Scots

ENGLAND

House of Wessex (England)

802–839	Egbert
839–858	Ethelwulf
858–860	Ethelbald
860–866	Ethelbert – first Christian king
866–871	Ethelred I
871–900	Alfred the Great
900–924	Edward I 'the Elder'
924–939	Athelstan – first king of all England
939–946	Edmund I
946–955	Edred
955–959	Edwig
957–975	Edgar
975–978	Edward II 'the Martyr'
978–1016	Ethelred II 'the Unready'
1016	Edmund II Ironside
1016–1035	King Canute (Danish king by conquest)
1035–1040	Harold I 'Harefoot'
1040–1043	Hardicanute
1042–1066	Edward III 'the Confessor'
1066	Harold II – killed at Hastings

House of Normandy

1066–1087	William I
1087–1100	William II
1100–1135	Henry I
1135–1154	Stephen

House of Plantagenet

1154–1189	Henry II
1189–1199	Richard I (also King of Jerusalem)
1199–1216	John
1216–1272	Henry III
1272–1307	Edward I
1307–1327	Edward II
1327–1377	Edward III
1377–1399	Richard II

The House of Lancaster

1399–1413	Henry IV
1413–1422	Henry V
1422–1461	Henry VI

House of York

1461–1483	Edward IV
1483	Edward V
1483–1485	Richard

House of Tudor

1485–1509	Henry VII
1509–1547	Henry VIII
1547–1553	Edward VI
1553–1558	Mary I
1558–1603	Elizabeth I

House of Stuart

1603–1625	James I (King of England and Scotland)
1625–1649	Charles I (King of England and Scotland)

Commonwealth and Protectorate

1649–1653	Government by a council of state
1653–1658	Protectorate of Oliver Cromwell
1658–1659	Protectorate of Richard Cromwell

House of Stuart (Restored)

1660–1685	Charles II (King of England and Scotland)
1685–1688	James II (King of England and Scotland)

House of Orange

1689–1694	William III and Mary II (jointly)
1694–1702	William III (sole ruler)
1702–1714	Anne (First Queen of Great Britain after Act of Union 1707.)

House of Hanover

1714–1727	George I (First King of Great Britain)
1727–1760	George II
1760–1820	George III
1820–1830	George IV
1830–1837	William IV
1837–1901	Victoria (First Empress of India)

House of Saxe-Coburg-Gotha

1901–1910	Edward VII (First Emperor of India)

House of Windsor

1910–1936	George V (Saxe-Coburg-Gotha until 1917)
1936	Edward VIII (abdicated)
1936–1952	George VI
1952–	Elizabeth II

King Canute
and Queen Aelgifu

You may find it easier to remember this rhyme. Memorise it and you'll use it and take satisfaction from the knowledge for the rest of your life.

> Willie, Willie, Harry, Steve,
> Harry, Dick, John, Harry Three,
> Edward One, Two, Three, Dick Two,
> Henry Four, Five, Six, then who?
> Edward Four, Five, Dick the Bad,
> Harrys twain and Ned the lad,
> Mary, Bessie, James you ken,
> Charlie, Charlie, James again.
> William and Mary, Anne of Gloria,
> Georges (4), Will Four, Victoria.
> Edward Seven, Georgie Five,
> Edward, George and Liz (alive).

Another excellent mnemonic is for Henry VIII's wives. In order, he married: Catherine of Aragon, Anne Boleyn, Jane Seymour, Anne of Cleves, Catherine Howard, and Catherine Parr. Their respective fates were: 'Divorced, beheaded, died, divorced, beheaded, survived.'

Henry VIII

THE LAWS OF FOOTBALL

Neatly enough, there are only seventeen main laws for the most popular game on earth. These are based on rules put together in England as far back as 1863 and formally ratified by the International Football Association Board in 1886.

1. **The pitch.** Length: 100–130 yds (90 m–120 m). Width: 50–100 yds (45 m–90 m). The two long lines are called touchlines, the two short lines are called goal lines. The pitch is divided by a halfway line, with a centre point where the 'kick-off' occurs to begin the match. At each goal, there is a 6-yard box (5.5 m) known as the goal area. Outside that, there is an 18-yard box (16.5 m) known as the penalty area. A penalty spot is drawn 12 yards (11 m) in front of the goalposts. The goalposts are 8 yards (7.32 m) apart and 8ft (2.44 m) high.

2. **The ball.** Circumference: between 27 and 28 inches (68–70 cm). Weight: between 14 and 16 oz (410–450 g).

3. **The teams.** No more than eleven players can be fielded by each team, including the goalkeeper. Depending on the competition, between three and seven substitutes can be used. In addition, any player can change places with the goalkeeper provided that the referee is

told and the change occurs while play has stopped.

4. **Clothing.** Players wear football shirts, shorts, shin-guards under long socks and football boots. Goalkeepers wear different-coloured kits.

5. **The referee.** All decisions by the referee are final. Powers include the ability to give a verbal warning, a more serious yellow card warning, or a red card, which results in immediate sending off. A second yellow card is equivalent to a red. The referee also acts as timekeeper for the match and controls any restarts after stopped play.

6. **Assistant referees** (linesmen). These indicate with a raised flag when a ball has crossed the lines and gone out of play, and let the referee know which side is to take the corner, goal kick, or throw-in. They also raise their flags to indicate when a player may be penalised for being in an offside position.

7. **Duration.** Two halves of forty-five minutes, with a half-time interval of no more than fifteen minutes.

8. **Starting.** Whichever team wins a coin-toss kicks off and begins play. The ball returns to the centre spot after a goal and at the start of the second half. All opposing players must be in their own half at kick-off – at least ten yards (9.15 m) from the ball.

9. **In and out.** The ball is out of play when it crosses any of the touchlines or goal lines, or if play has been stopped by the referee. It is in play at all other times.

10. **Scoring.** The whole ball has to pass over the goal line. If a member of the defending team knocks it in by accident, it is an 'own goal' and still valid. Whoever scores the most goals wins.

11. **Offside.** The offside rule is designed to stop players hanging around the goal of their opponents, waiting for a long ball to come to them. A player is given offside if the ball is passed to him while he is nearer to the goal than the ball and the second-last defender. Note that players are allowed to sit on the goal line if they want, but the ball cannot come to them without offside being called by the referee. An 'offside trap' is when defenders deliberately move up the field to leave a forward player in a position where he cannot take the ball without being called offside. It is not an offside offence if the ball comes to a player from a throw-in, a goal kick or a corner kick.

12. **Fouls.** Direct and indirect free kicks can be given to the opposing team if the referee judges a foul has been committed. The kick is taken from where the foul occurred, so if it is close to the opponent's goal, the game can easily hinge on the outcome. Fouls can range from touching the ball with the hands to kicking

an opponent. In addition, the player can be cautioned or sent off depending on the offence.

13. **Free kicks.** Direct free kicks can be a shot at goal if the spot is close enough, so are given for more serious fouls. The ball is stationary when kicked. Opposing players are not allowed closer than ten yards (9.15 m), which has come to mean in practice that the opposing team put a wall of players ten yards from the spot to obscure the kicker's vision.

Indirect free kicks cannot be directly at goal, but must first be passed to another player.

14. **Penalties.** These are awarded for the same offences as direct free kicks – if the offence happens inside the penalty area of the opposing team. This is to prevent what are known as 'professional fouls', where an attacker is brought down deliberately to stop him scoring.

The goalkeeper must remain on his goal line between the posts until the ball has been kicked. Other players must be outside the penalty area and at least ten yards from the penalty spot – that's why there's an arc on the penalty area.

The penalty must be a single strike at the goal. As long as it goes in, it can hit the posts and/or goalkeeper as well. In the normal run of play, a penalty kick that rebounds off the keeper is back in play and can be struck again. In a penalty shootout, this does not apply and there is only one chance to score.

15. **Throw-ins.** A player must face inwards to the field and have both feet on the ground, on or behind the touchline. Both hands must be used and the ball must be delivered from behind the head. The thrower must pass the ball to another player before he can touch it again.

16. **Goal kicks.** These are given when the opposing team kick the ball over the opposing goal line, after a missed shot at goal, for example. The goal kick is taken from anywhere within the goal area and the ball must pass out of the penalty area before another player can touch it.

17. **Corner kicks.** These are given when a member of the defending team knocks the ball over his own goal line. The goalkeeper may do this in the process of saving a goal, for example, or a defender may do it quite deliberately to prevent a shot reaching goal. Many goals are scored from corner kicks, so the tension is always high when one is given.

Defending players must remain at least ten yards (9.15 m) from the ball until it is kicked. In practice, they group themselves around the goalmouth. Defenders work hard to prevent attackers finding a free space. Attackers work to drop their marking defender, get the ball as it comes in and either head or kick it into the goal. A goalkeeper is hard-pressed during corners. Visibility is reduced due to the number of people involved and the ball can come from almost anywhere with very little time to react.

OTHER POINTS OF INTEREST

The goalkeeper is the only player able to use his hands. However, apart from the lower arms and hands, any other part of the body can be used to help control the ball.

If the game must be played to a conclusion (in a World Cup, for example), extra time can be given. There are various forms of this, but it usually involves two halves of fifteen minutes each. If the scores are still tied at the end of extra time, a penalty shootout is used to decide the winner. Five pre-arranged players take it in turns to shoot at the goal. If the scores are *still* tied, it goes to sudden-death penalties, one after the other until a winner is found.

One advantage that football has over rugby and cricket is the fact that if you have a wall, you can practise football forever. The other games really need someone else. There are many ball skills that must be experienced to be learned. It's all very well reading that you can bend the ball from right to left in the air by striking the bottom half of the right side of the ball with the inside of your foot, or left to right by using the outside of your foot on the bottom half of the left side of the ball. Realistically though, to make it work, you'll have to spend many, many hours practising. This is true of any sport – and for that matter any skill of any kind. If you want to be good at something, do it regularly. It's an old, old phrase, but 'use makes master' is as true today as it was hundreds of years ago. Natural-born skill is all very well, but it will only take you so far against someone who has practised every day at something he loves.

MARBLING PAPER

IF YOU'VE EVER WONDERED how the marbled paper inside the covers of old books is created, here it is. It is a surprisingly simple process, but the results can be very impressive. Once you have the inks, there are all sorts of possibilities, like birthday wrapping paper or your own greeting cards.

You will need

- Marbling ink – available from any craft or hobby shop and some large stationers.
- A flat-bottomed tray – a baking tray for example.
- A4 paper for printing and newspaper ready to lay out the wet sheets.
- Small paintbrush, a toothpick, comb or feather to swirl ink.

At about £3.50 a pot, marbling ink is expensive, but you only need a tiny amount for each sheet, so they last for years. We began with red, blue and gold.

We used A4 printer paper as it was handy, but almost any blank paper will do. You could do this in the bath, but remember to clean it later or you will have a blue father or mother the following morning. The paper must not have a shiny surface, or the inks won't penetrate.

1. Fill the tray with water to the depth of about an inch (25 mm). It is not necessary to be exact.
2. Using the small brush, or a dropper, touch the first colour to the water surface. It will spread immediately in widening circles.
3. Speckle the water with circles of your colours, then when you are satisfied, swirl the colours with a toothpick, a comb or a feather. Anything with a point will do for the first attempt.
4. When the pattern is ready, place the sheet of paper face down onto it and wait for sixty seconds. That is long enough for printer paper, though times may vary with different types.
5. Take hold of one end of the paper and draw it upwards out of the liquid. There really isn't any way to do this incorrectly, as far as we could tell – it really is easy. Wash your paper under the tap to get rid of excess ink. Place the wet sheet on newspaper and leave to dry.

If you have access to a colour photocopier or printer, you could make a copy with certain sections blanked off. The spaces could then be used for invitation details, or the title of a diary or story – perhaps an old-fashioned Victorian ghost story, with an old-fashioned marble-paper cover. Dark green, gold and black is a great combination.

RIDDLES

RIDDLES ARE FIENDISH puzzles, usually set in words. In ancient times, King Solomon used them to test the wits of friends and enemies – and had his own tested in the same way by the queen of Sheba. In the Bible, Samson saw a bee-hive in the body of a dead lion. He ate the meat and honey and posed this riddle to his enemies: 'Out of the eater came meat. Out of the strong came forth sweetness.'

History is full of interesting examples of the form. According to the Greek historian Plutarch, Homer apparently died from frustration when he could not solve the riddle of the fishermen of Ios. That riddle is below.

Another Greek example was a physical puzzle. The Gordian knot was a huge nest of twisted bark in a great ball, with no ends showing. An oracle had predicted that the man who loosed the knot would rule all of Asia. When

Alexander the Great came upon the shrine that housed the knot, he solved the problem by taking his sword and cutting it in half, fulfilling the prophecy.

Perhaps the most famous of all is the Riddle of the Sphinx. In Greek mythology, the Sphinx was a huge lion with the head of a ram, falcon or a man. When travellers came upon the beast, it would ask its riddle and if they could not answer, it would kill them.

All the answers are below, but take a little time to consider the riddles first.

1. The Riddle of the Sphinx

    'What goes on four legs in the morning, two legs in the afternoon and three legs in the evening?'

    Oedipus was the Greek hero who solved the riddle and the Sphinx destroyed herself in rage.

2. The Riddle put to Homer by the fishermen of Ios

    'What we caught we threw away; what we didn't catch, we kept.'

3. A riddle of ancient Greece, the author anonymous

    'I am the black child of a white father;
    A wingless bird, flying even to the clouds of heaven.
    I give birth to tears of mourning in pupils that meet me,
    and at once on my birth I am dissolved into air.'

4. Around a hundred Anglo-Saxon riddles survive. Some come from *Beowulf* which was written in the 'middle ages' between the fifth and 10th centuries. They were not meant to be set and answered quickly, but rather mulled over. Here are three good ones.

   i) 'The creature ate its words. It seemed to me strangely weird when I heard this wonder: that it devoured human speech. A thief in the darkness, gloriously mouthed the source of knowledge. But the thief was not wiser, for all the words in his mouth.'

   ii) 'When I am alive I do not speak.
       Anyone who wants to takes me captive and cuts off my head.
       They bite my bare body
       I do no harm to anyone unless they cut me first.
       Then I soon make them cry.'

   iii) 'I am all on my own,
        Wounded by iron weapons and scarred by swords.
        I often see battle.
        I am tired of fighting.
        I do not expect to be allowed to retire from warfare
        Before I am completely done for.
        At the wall of the city, I am knocked about
        And bitten again and again.

Hard edged things made by the blacksmith's
    hammer attack me.
Each time I wait for something worse.
I have never been able to find a doctor who could
    make me better
Or give me medicine made from herbs.
Instead the sword gashes all over me grow bigger
    day and night.'

5. This one is much later, written by the author of *Gulliver's Travels*, Jonathan Swift (1667–1745).

'Begotten, and Born, and dying with Noise,
The Terror of Women, and Pleasure of Boys,
Like the Fiction of Poets concerning the Wind,
I'm chiefly unruly, when strongest confin'd.
For Silver and Gold I don't trouble my Head,
But all I delight in is Pieces of Lead;
Except when I trade with a Ship or a Town,
Why then I make pieces of Iron go down.
One Property more I would have you remark,
No Lady was ever more fond of a Spark;
The Moment I get one my Soul's all a-fire,
And I roar out my Joy, and in Transport expire.'

6. Later still, is this one by William Davidson (1781–1858)

'My sides are firmly lac'd about,
Yet nothing is within;

You'll think my head is strange indeed,
Being nothing else but skin.'

7. As a final example, here is a riddle said to be written by Albert Einstein in the late nineteenth century. It is extremely complex, but there are no tricks. Cold logic will solve it, though Einstein apparently estimated that only 2% of humanity would have the intelligence to find the answer. You might like to try it on a maths teacher.

   1. In a street there are five houses, painted five different colours.
   2. In each house lives a person of different nationality.
   3. These five homeowners each drink a different kind of beverage, smoke a different brand of cigar and keep a different pet.

The question is: Who owns the fish?

Clues:

   1. The Brit lives in a red house.
   2. The Swede keeps dogs as pets.
   3. The Dane drinks tea.
   4. The Green house is next to, and on the left of the White house.
   5. The owner of the Green house drinks coffee.
   6. The person who smokes Pall Mall rears birds.
   7. The owner of the Yellow house smokes Dunhill.

8. The man living in the centre house drinks milk.

9. The Norwegian lives in the first house.

10. The man who smokes Blends lives next to the one who keeps cats.

11. The man who keeps horses lives next to the man who smokes Dunhill.

12. The man who smokes Blue Master drinks beer.

13. The German smokes Prince.

14. The Norwegian lives next to the blue house.

15. The man who smokes Blends has a neighbour who drinks water.

Answers:

1. A man – who crawls as a baby, walks as a man and then uses a stick as an old fellow.

2. The fishermen had lice.

3. Smoke

4 i) A bookworm, or a moth ii) An onion iii) A shield.

5. A cannon.

6. A drum.

7. You're going to need to draw a grid for this one. It is a process of elimination and slowly building a picture of what we know. For example, the Brit lives in a red house and the owner of the Yellow house smokes Dunhill – so we know the Brit cannot smoke Dunhill. As you can see from the grid, it is the German who owns the fish.

	House 1	House 2	House 3	House 4	House 5
Colour	Yellow	Blue	Red	Green	White
Nationality	Norwegian	Dane	Brit	German	Swede
Drink	Water	Tea	Milk	Coffee	Beer
Smokes	Dunhill	Blends	Pall Mall	Prince	Blue Mast
Pet	Cat	Horses	Birds	Fish	Dogs

THE BRITISH EMPIRE
(1497–1997):

'The empire on which the sun never sets'

FIVE CENTURIES of energy, triumph and disaster, heroism and invention are too full to be explored here in the detail they deserve. What follows is a summary of the rise and fall of the largest empire the world has ever known. The influence of language, custom, law and tradition continues, but the British Empire came to an end on 30 June 1997, when Hong Kong passed back into Chinese ownership. It is astonishing to think that almost exactly 100 years before, on 20 June 1897, Queen Victoria celebrated her Diamond Jubilee of sixty years ruling 375 million subjects. The idea that the Empire would vanish only a century later would have been laughed at, though Rudyard Kipling saw that the world turns on, regardless of human achievement. His poem 'Recessional' was read to Victoria. These four lines are particularly poignant.

> *Far-called, our navies melt away –*
> *On dune and headland sinks the fire –*
> *Lo, all our pomp of yesterday*
> *Is one with Nineveh, and Tyre!*

It has struck some that if an empire had to be broken against an enemy, Nazi Germany was a worthy cause. All the countries in the Empire sent men back for that conflict. They came from America, India, Canada, Nepal, New Zealand, Australia, South Africa – everywhere, in fact, where the people could claim a bond with Britain – to give their lives against a dark and terrible enemy. Perhaps that was the purpose of the British Empire – to be there at that time, when the future could have gone another way. As a legacy, perhaps that will do.

On 20 May 1497, John Cabot set sail from Bristol with a royal warrant to claim land for Henry VII. This was the first document of what would one day become the Empire.

He made landfall in Newfoundland, on the north-eastern edge of Canada. His son Sebastian established the Company of Merchant Adventurers in London and secured a trade treaty with Ivan the Terrible in Russia. English trade interests were beginning to grow, and by the time of Elizabeth I they would come into conflict with the ambitions of Spain. There were several reasons for the rivalry. The Spanish royals had sponsored Christopher Columbus, they were Catholic where Elizabeth was Protestant, and most importantly of all, the two growing trade fleets competed against each other. English pirates would capture Spanish ships laden with gold, silver and slaves from their colonies in South America. In turn, English crews would be arrested and tortured whenever the opportunity presented itself. It was a brutal period, with fortunes for the taking, which helped to establish the English as a naval nation. Elizabeth I even leased ships to privateers in exchange for a tithe of the profits. It was simple: it rewarded daring and it brought vast wealth to Britain. As Sir Walter Raleigh said,

> Whosoever commands the sea commands the trade; whosoever commands the trade of the world commands the riches of the world and consequently the world itself.

Sir Francis Drake had first sailed with the privateer John Hawkins, a scourge of merchant shipping. In his turn, Drake became the most notorious of privateer captains, taking great pleasure in attacks on Spanish vessels. He saw the 'Papist' Catholic Spanish as enemies to a Protestant England and was happy to ambush their ships and even a mule-train carrying silver from Peru to Panama. He became a popular hero in England and was a dashing favourite of the Queen. He was the second man to circumnavigate the globe (after Magellan) – though he missed finding the legendary southern continent

Sir Francis Drake

(Australia) – and reached California, naming it New Albion. He brought his queen £160,000 profit from just one voyage – in a day when a man could live comfortably on £20 a year. He was knighted on the quarterdeck of his ship, the *Golden Hind*.

When he heard the Spanish were preparing a great armada in Cadiz, Drake took fifty ships out to attack them with fire-ships before they could sail out of the harbour. His fleet did so much damage that the Spanish took a year to rebuild. Drake said that he had 'merely singed the King of Spain's beard', but Elizabeth would not agree to further attacks.

In 1588, the Spanish Armada sailed into the English Channel. Many of the Spanish ships were lost to strong winds and high seas, leading King Philip to comment later that 'God is an Englishman.' In addition to natural forces, the Spanish fleet was beaten by faster gunnery, nimbler ships and better captains, ending the likelihood that the future would be Spanish-led.

This was to be the hallmark of the early British Empire. Trade would drive its expansion, then war, almost always with European nations seeking their own wealth. Over the next four centuries, Britain would go to war with almost every European country. Perhaps because of Europe being a cauldron of conflict for the previous three thousand years, the nations of the continent were superior to the rest of the world in terms of arms, tactics, ships, technology and materials such as steel. Holland, France, Spain, Germany and Britain all exploded outwards, using their advantages to win territories and profit. One by one, all of the others were beaten home again. The French were finally stopped at Waterloo and the Germans in 1945. The Empire would eventually become the Commonwealth, in a peaceful transition, as the world headed towards the third millennium.

When James VI of Scotland combined the thrones to become King of England, Scotland and Ireland in 1603, the new century would provide fresh challenges for the nascent Empire.

In 1613, the East India Trading Company established its first settlement at Surat in India. Their aim was to grow spices in competition with Dutch traders. Exploration and adventure led the way, with men such as Captain John Smith, who named New England, and Sir George Somers, who discovered Bermuda when he was blown off course.

King James was a Presbyterian (of the Church of Scotland) and Puritans in England were deeply unhappy with his rule. In 1620, a disaffected group of them set sail from Southampton in two ships – the *Speedwell* and the *Mayflower*. The *Speedwell* was unseaworthy and they both turned back to Plymouth. The *Mayflower* then went out alone, carrying Puritans, crew and colonists recruited by the Virginia Trading Company. They made landfall first in Cape Cod, but could find no decent shelter in the depths of a hostile winter. The second landing was at Plymouth in Massachusetts, named so previously by Captain John Smith. Many more would follow and over time Maine, New Hampshire and Connecticut were settled. The new world was opening up and by 1630, Boston and ten other settlements were established. By 1643, New Haven, Plymouth, Connecticut and Massachusetts formed a confederation as the United Colonies of New England.

In England, Charles I had taken the throne and actually lost it in the English Civil War with Oliver Cromwell. The American colonies began to taste their own freedom from the mother country. In 1688 William of Orange was asked by the English parliament to take the throne from James II, who was once again insisting England should become Catholic. William had a claim to the throne through being a grandson of Charles I and he landed with an honour guard, after James II had gone into exile in France. The Crown's grip on the American colonies became oppressive during his reign.

In 1707, the kingdoms of England and Scotland were legally and politically joined by the Act of Union, an important part of British history. Gibraltar (at the southern tip of Spain) became a British port in perpetuity by the Treaty of Utrecht in 1713. Minorca was also turned over to Britain but, more importantly, France was forced to drop her claim to vast territories in Canada. However, it would take military action to enforce British sovereignty over Canada. Even while a new capital was being built in 1748, French attacks on British settlements continued. Eventually, the French colonists were given the choice of swearing allegiance to the British Crown or being deported. Most chose to be deported.

In America, the struggle between France and Britain continued. A French expedition took control of the Ohio Valley and a messenger named George Washington was sent to tell them to withdraw. His small unit was made to surrender by the French. A much larger army that included 1,200 regular soldiers from Britain would be almost annihilated by a combined French and Iroquois Indian force. The rebellion spread, though this particular force was eventually routed and driven back. In 1756, the Seven

Years War with France began and in America, Canada and India, as well as closer to home, French and British forces fought bitter battles.

✳

Robert Clive of India might have remained an East India Company clerk if not for the war. Famously he had tried to commit suicide twice, failing both times with a jamming gun. He was made an ensign in the Company army and became almost the archetype of that strange breed Britain could produce – men with an absolute disregard for personal safety and an unshakeable belief in the rightness of their cause. The Mahrattas of India called Clive 'Sabat Jung' – 'Daring in War'.

Calcutta was begun as a settlement by the British East India Company. The Company officials fortified their base in Calcutta against local insurrection. The

Robert Clive

Nabob of Bengal decided this was an act of defiance and sent a great host against the fort, overwhelming it. The 146 company employees surrendered on the condition that their lives be spared. They were held without water in a stifling room twenty-four feet by eighteen. In the morning, only twenty-three had survived what became known as 'the black hole of Calcutta'.

It could all have been lost in 1756. The French were growing in strength in India, while the East India Company had lost Calcutta and Madras. British colonies in America seemed vulnerable to French attack. In addition, Britain lost Minorca and Spain entered the war on the side of France in 1762.

In England, the Prime Minister, William Pitt (Pitt the Elder), came up with the idea of funding the Prussian army to wage war against the French-led alliance of Austria, Russia, Saxony, Sweden and Spain, allowing Britain to concentrate her troops in far-flung places such as India and Canada. He was particularly lucky in having Frederick the Great as his ally, as the man was a tactical genius. The Seven Years War can be considered the first world war, given the scale of it. It is still the most successful war ever fought by Britain as it brought India and Canada into the fold and practically began an empire overnight. Pitt did not lack confidence: 'I know that I can save this country and no one else can,' he said.

Clive recaptured Calcutta in 1757 and after extraordinary subterfuge and negotiation, fought the Battle of Plassey against a French and Indian army of 50,000 with fifty-three guns. Clive had 1,100 British troops, 2,100 natives and ten guns. The French gunners continued fighting right to the end, but Clive's force routed the enemy and secured Bengal for British rule. It has been said that Plassey was the turning point, but in fact there were hundreds of times and places where the British Empire could have failed. Only when we look back with an Olympian perspective does it seem inevitable. For those involved in its creation, every year survived was a gift and only luck, fortitude, bravery and cunning could hold it for the year after that.

In Canada, Pitt was fortunate to have another gifted soldier – James Wolfe. The fleet took an expeditionary force of 9,000 British regulars and 500 colonials from Halifax to take Louisburg and then Quebec from the French. In 1758, Wolfe led the attack on Louisburg carrying only a cane. The guns of the great fort were taken and turned on French ships in harbour. The first step had been taken to pushing the French out of Canada. However, the fighting was ferocious as fort after fort was captured throughout 1759.

Wolfe was made major general and took command for the assault on Quebec, an almost impregnable fortress above the St Lawrence river. (James Cook was the surveyor of the river, the man who later went on to claim Australia and map New Zealand.) The night before, Wolfe gave a locket to John Jervis, a naval captain, to be sent to his fiancée if he died. As an admiral, Jervis would later play a crucial role in Nelson's career and lived until 1823.

'The Death of Wolfe' by Benjamin West.

Wolfe's army fought the French on 13 September 1759 on the Plains of Abraham in front of the city. Both commanders were mortally wounded. Wolfe died during the battle and the French commander later that night. Quebec surrendered and the British garrisoned the city.

There were other battles, but on 8 September 1760, the French surrendered their interest in Canada. They had lost fleets to British ships and Britain was free from the threat of invasion. Bells rang in London to celebrate a year of victories.

✳

The American War of Independence could also have been the beginning of the end. In a very real sense, this was a civil war between British forces who wanted to remain loyal to Britain and others who wanted to forge their own identity as a separate country rather than one ruled from abroad. The causes are complex, though part of the rea son for the war was the level of taxes imposed by Britain on such products as sugar and, most famously, tea. 'No taxation without representation' was the cry raised against King George III. The cry, needless to say, was ignored and further taxes were imposed on glass, lead, paper and just about anything else the British government could think of. Riots followed in America and bloodshed was inevitable. A change of government in Britain meant that all taxes were repealed except for the one on tea, but it was too late and in 1773 in Boston 342 boxes of tea worth £10,000 were tipped into the harbour – known ever after as 'the Boston tea party'.

Britain had reduced the size of the army after the Seven Years War. Clive had at last managed to shoot himself, Wolfe was dead and Pitt was too elderly and frail to help the situation. George III suffered from porphyria, a disease that rendered him completely insane for temporary peri ods. From 1773 to 1783, Britain needed a great negotiator, a visionary, or possibly a Wellington or a Nelson. For once, there wasn't one and the war was a shambles. Interest ingly, the French played a crucial part, still smarting from their defeat in the Seven Years War. Apart from providing supplies, France formed a league of 'armed neutrality' with Spain, Russia, Prussia, Holland and Sweden to protect American shipping from the Royal Navy. A French fleet brought 5,000 men and 106 heavy guns from Toulon to support their General Lafayette in America. After landing the army, the French fleet attacked British ships waiting for a retreating British force under Cornwallis. With his back to the sea, Cornwallis was forced to surrender at Yorktown. Famously, his military band played 'The world turned upside down'. In September 1783, Britain recognised the independence of the thirteen American states. George Washington became the first president six years later on 30 April 1789 – the year of the French Revolution. Napoleon Bonaparte had arrived on the world scene.

Canada remained a British possession, though limited autonomy was given soon after the American war and perhaps because of it. India was thriving to the point where the British government wanted more influence, and Pitt the Younger passed a law that gave the government oversight control of the East India Company in 1784. India had become the jewel in the Crown, though the Company was a force in the country for another hundred years. Trade continued to grow, though Britain abolished slavery in 1807 and then used the navy to enforce the abolition on the shipping of all other countries.

Napoleon was eventually beaten by an alliance led by Wellington on land, and Nelson's Royal Navy at sea. The Treaty of Vienna in 1815 effectively ended the threat of France to British interests. Parts of north Africa and a number of small islands remain under French control to this day, but the possibility of the world speaking French had passed. Even time would be measured through Greenwich rather than Paris, though the one place in the world that does not recognise Greenwich Mean Time is the part of France directly south of Greenwich. Perhaps unsurprisingly, they keep continental time – one hour ahead.

※

As the Victorian era began in 1837, the Empire continued to expand. Dutch Boers had established settlements in south Africa by the beginning of the nineteenth century and Britain developed its own outposts in that rich land, though the Boer Wars didn't come till later. Hong Kong was gained by treaty with China in 1839 after trade wars over opium, tea and silver. In 1840, Britain claimed New Zealand and fought the warrior Maoris over the land for the next thirty years. In 1848, Britain made Canada largely self-governing and when that was successful, used the same formula in Australia and New Zealand. This was the seed of the Commonwealth. In 1867, Britain united all the Canadian provinces into one dominion – one country. Afghanistan was occupied and then lost. India had railways, schools and hospitals built across it as part of a complex infrastructure. The Punjab was annexed after wars with the Sikhs, who earned the respect of the British with their courage and tenacity. Tea was introduced as a crop in India and Ceylon (Sri Lanka) by the British, intent on breaking the Chinese tea monopoly.

The Indian Mutiny of 1857 occurred when Sepoy soldiers rebelled against the imposition of British culture. For

THE BRITISH EMPIRE (1497–1997)

example, female infanticide had been outlawed and 'suttee', the practice of burning a live widow with her dead husband, was also banned. Attempts to emancipate women did not go down well and the spread of Christianity in India was seen as a threat to Islam and Hinduism.

Famously, the mutiny was set off by a rumour that the British rifle cartridges had been greased with pig and cow fat and were therefore untouchable to Hindus and Muslims. Indian regiments refused the cartridges and mutinied, murdering the white officers and rioting in a great release of horror and violence. British forces were heavily outnumbered by native troops they had trained and were besieged and massacred. The Gurkhas of Nepal and the Sikhs of the Punjab remained loyal. The Siege of Cawnpore was particularly brutal. Safe passage had been promised to a thousand men, women and children. They had barricaded themselves into the small fort for twenty days against an army of ten thousand. When they came out, they were massacred. Five hundred and six children were hacked to pieces and thrown into a well. The British who came too late to relieve them were filled with rage at what they saw. Other atrocities followed, such as the British strapping Sepoys to the mouths of cannons as they were fired. The battles were fierce and brutal, with 182 Victoria Crosses being awarded for courage. Only the First World War would produce more examples of extraordinary heroism (181 were awarded in WWII, 626 in WWI).

Sir Colin Campbell, Sir Hugh Rose and Sir James Outram eventually broke the rebellion and India slipped

back into an uneasy peace. The country would not become independent until 1947, after the Second World War.

Victoria's reign ended in 1901, with the Empire still growing. Germany and Austria would be the chief enemy in the new century, though France was always willing to take on new colonies if an opportunity presented itself. South Africa was the first battleground of the century, with Britain clashing with the Dutch over rights to the continent.

Some acquisitions, like the Transvaal in south Africa, were claimed in part to disrupt the power base of other countries before they became a threat. Nonetheless, political decisions had to be carried out by the army and navy, fighting the Dutch Boers.

World War I (1914–18) was fought at sea and on every continent, with Britain leading a block of allies against another block led by Germany. It does not need to be said that millions of lives were lost in the most brutal of conditions. The Germans under Kaiser Wilhelm were beaten after four years of war and the guns in France fell silent at eleven in the morning, on the eleventh day of the eleventh month, 1918. 'Remembrance Day' is still marked every year with memorial services and the sale of poppies.

Former German colonies in Africa became British possessions, such as Cameroon, Togoland and East Africa. In addition, Iraq and Palestine became 'British Mandates', which meant Britain assumed responsibility for them, as well as adding Egypt, Cyprus, Kuwait, the Sudan and a host of other small states. With France on the winning side, Syria and Lebanon became French colonies. In all, nearly two million square miles were added to the Empire and when Britain laid claim to Antarctica in 1919, the Empire was the largest it had ever been.

※

The Victorian era had produced many who saw the Empire as theirs by divine right. The drive to spread civilisation produced missionaries and reformers like Florence Nightingale and William Wilberforce, who campaigned against slavery. Gentlemen adventurers were the archetypal example of young Christians who were prepared to risk their lives for more than the simple fortunes of Drake and Ralegh's time. The dream had altered to one that brought the light of British rule to those less fortunate, making the world a better place as a result. The British assumed a moral superiority as well as a financial and military one. The result was a spread of culture that altered the world for ever.

Characters like Cecil Rhodes, who ruled what is now known as Zimbabwe, calling it Rhodesia, were from the same mould as Richard Francis Burton, T.E. Lawrence, James Brooke, Kitchener, Napier and a thousand other examples of the breed. Their achievements are astonishing in scale and breathtaking self-confidence. At the same time, Britain produced a stream of reformers and more liberal thinkers who stood against the brutal treatment of native populations and deplored acts of violence. Both types created an Empire capable of merciless ferocity in places like Ireland and India – and a humanitarian philosophy that led to improved health and education for its subjects. As Mahatma Ghandi said in 1915,

> I discovered that the British Empire had certain ideals with which I had fallen in love. One of those ideals is that every subject of the British Empire has the freest scope possible for his energies and efforts and whatever he thinks is due to his conscience... I have said that government is best which governs least, and I have found it possible for me to be governed least under the British Empire. Hence my loyalty to the British Empire.

The idea of a 'Nightwatchman' state, that is one that that does not interfere in every aspect of people's lives, was a peculiarly British idea, quite different from the governments of the continent. It came about because the vast Empire simply could not be governed on the sort of scale that is possible today.

The years between the wars are generally regarded as a golden period by those who lived through them. The *Boy's Own Paper* gives an idea of the attitudes of the day, valuing attributes of manliness, fair play, decency, honour and an ability to play cricket. The idea that the century would see the end of British rule over almost all of it would have been preposterous. Yet, the Second World War was fought to resist the military rise of Germany – carrying with it a quite different and darker philosophy.

As Niall Ferguson said in his book *Empire: How Britain Made the Modern World*:

TOGETHER

When the British governed a country – even when they only influenced its government by flexing their military and financial muscles – there were certain distinctive features of their own society that they tended to disseminate. A list of the more important of these would run:

1 The English language
2. English forms of land tenure
3. Scottish and English banking
4. The Common Law
5. Protestantism
6. Team sports
7. The limited or 'Nightwatchman' state
8. Representative assemblies
9. The idea of liberty.

The last of these is perhaps the most important because it remains the most distinctive feature of the Empire, the thing that sets it apart from its continental European rivals. I do not mean to claim that all British Imperialists were liberals: some were very far from it. But what is striking about the history of the Empire is that whenever the British were behaving despotically, there was almost always a liberal critique of that behaviour from within British society.

UNDERSTANDING GRAMMAR – PART ONE

———— ✠ ————

IT'S STRANGE HOW SATISFYING it can be to know right from wrong. Grammar is all about rules and structure. It is *always* 'between you and me', for example. If you hear someone say 'between you and I', it isn't a matter of opinion, they're just wrong.

The grammar of English is more complex than can be contained here, but a skeleton of basics is well within our reach. You wouldn't use a chisel without knowing how to hold it. In the same way, you really should know the sharp end from the blunt one in everything else you use – including your language. The English language is spoken by more people on earth than any other, after all.

The first thing to know is that there are only nine kinds of words. Nine.

⤳ Nouns ⤳

1. **Nouns** are the names of things. There are three kinds. Proper nouns have capital letters e.g. 'Newcastle'. Abstract nouns are the things that exist but you can't touch: 'courage', 'loyalty', 'cruelty', 'kindness'. Common nouns are the words for everything else: 'chair', 'eyes', 'dog', 'car' and so on.

⌒ **Verbs** ⌒

2. **Verbs** are words for action or change: 'to become', 'to wash', 'to dissect', 'to eat' and so on. There are six parts to each verb, known as first person singular, second person singular, third person singular, first person plural, second person plural and third person plural.

   Most verbs follow this simple pattern.

To deliver

First person singular:	*I deliver*
Second person singular:	*You deliver*
Third person singular:	*He/She/It delivers* – note the 's'
First person plural:	*We deliver*
Second person plural:	*You deliver*
Third person plural:	*They deliver*

Irregular verbs like 'to be' and 'to have' are not as... well, not as regular. They must be learned.

To be	**To have**
I am	I have
You are	You have
He/She/It is	He/She/It has
We are	We have
You are	You have
They are	They have

Note that the second person 'you' is the same in the singular and plural. In older forms of English, you would have used 'thou' as second person singular. In modern English it makes no difference whether you are addressing one man or a thousand, you could still begin as follows: 'You are responsible for your behaviour.'

∽ Adverbs ∽

3. **Adverbs** are the words that modify verbs, adjectives and other adverbs. They are important as there is a huge difference between 'smiling nastily' and 'smiling cheerfully'. Clearly the verb is not enough on its own.

Most adverbs end in '-ly', as with the examples above.

If you say, 'I'll go to the shops tomorrow,' however, 'tomorrow' is an adverb, because it adds detail to that verb 'go'. Words like 'soon' and 'often' also fall into this category. As a group, these are sometimes known as 'adverbs of time'.

As mentioned above, an adverb can also add detail to an adjective. 'It is really big' uses 'really' as an adverb. 'It is very small' uses 'very' as an adverb. He walked 'extremely quietly' uses 'extremely' as an adverb for an adverb! This is not rocket science. Take it slowly and learn it all bit by bit.

∽ Adjectives ∽

4   **Adjectives** are words that modify nouns. In 'the enormous snake', 'enormous' is the adjective. More than one can be used together, thus: 'the small, green snake'. Note the comma between the two adjectives. Putting a comma between adjectives is correct.

   As a general rule, adjectives come before the noun. However, as always with English, rules have many exceptions: 'That snail is *slimy*!', for example.

∽ Pronouns ∽

5.   **Pronouns** are words that replace nouns in a sentence. It would sound clumsy to say 'John looked in John's pockets.' Instead, we say 'John looked in *his* pockets'. 'His' is a pronoun.

   Here are some examples: *I, you, he, she, we, they – me, you, him, her, us, them – my, your, his, her, our, their*

   'One' is also used in place of 'people in general', as in the following sentence: 'One should always invest in reliable stocks.' The informal form of this is 'you', but it does sometimes lead to confusion, which keeps this unusual use of 'one' alive. The Queen also uses the 'we' form in place of 'I' during formal announcements.

⟾ Conjunction ⟾

6. A **conjunction** is a word that joins parts of a sentence together. 'I tied the knot and hoped for the best.' Tying the knot is a separate action to hoping for the best, joined by the word 'and'. Conjunctions can also join adjectives, 'short and snappy', or adverbs 'slowly but surely'.

Examples: *and, so, but, or, if, although, though, because, since, when, as, whilst, nor.*

The general rule is: 'A sentence does not begin with a conjunction.' Yes, you will find examples where sentences do begin with a conjunction. Professional writers do break this rule, but you should know it to break it – and even then do it carefully.

The examples above are fairly straightforward. It does get a little trickier when a conjunction is used to introduce a subordinate clause. (Clauses are covered in Grammar Part Two.)

'Although he was my only friend, I hated him.' (Although)

'As I'm here, I'll have a drink.' (As).

In these two examples, the sentences have been rearranged to change the emphasis. It would have been clearer, perhaps, to write, 'I'll have a drink as I'm here', or 'I hated him although he was my only friend.' It's easier to see 'although' and 'as' are being used as joining words in that way, but many sentences begin with a subordinate clause.

❦ Articles ❧

7. **Articles** are perhaps the easiest to remember: 'a', 'an' and 'the'. That's it.

   'A/an' is the **indefinite** article. Used when an object is unknown. 'A dog is in my garden.' 'An elephant is sitting on my father.'

   'The' is the **definite** article. 'The dog is in the garden' can refer to a particular dog. 'The elephant is sitting on my father' can mean only one elephant – one we already know: a family pet, perhaps.

   'An' is still sometimes used for words that begin with a clearly sounded 'h': 'an historical battle', 'an horrendous evil' and so on. It is seen as old-fashioned, though, and using 'a' is becoming more acceptable.

❦ Prepositions ❧

8. **Prepositions** are words that mark the position or relationship of one thing with respect to another. Examples: *in, under, over, between, before, behind, through, above, for, with, at and from.*

   'He fell from grace' demonstrates 'from' as a preposition. Another example is 'He lived *before* Caesar', or 'I stood *with* Caesar.'

   The general rule for prepositions is: 'Don't end a sentence with a preposition.'

   It is not correct to say 'This is my son, who I am most

pleased with.' It should be 'This is my son, with whom I am most pleased.'

⌒ **Interjections** ⌒

9. This is another of the easier types. **Interjections** are simple sounds used to express an inward feeling such as sorrow, surprise, pain or anger. This can be a wide group, as almost anything can be said in this way. Obvious examples are: *Oh! What? Hell! Eh? Goodness gracious!*

Note the last one – interjections don't have to be a single word. It could be a whole phrase like 'By the Lord Harry!' or a complex oath. They tend to stand on their own and often have exclamation marks following them.

That is all nine.

Bearing in mind that English has more words than any other language on earth, it is quite impressive that there are only nine kinds. The first part of grammar is to learn those nine well and be able to identify them in a sentence. If you have, you should be able to name each of the eight kinds of words used in the following sentence. If it helps, we didn't use a conjunction.

'No! I saw the old wolf biting viciously at his leg.'

(Answer: 'No!' – interjection, 'I' – pronoun, 'saw' – verb, 'the' – definite article, 'old' – adjective, 'wolf' – common noun, 'biting' – verb, 'viciously' – adverb, 'at' – preposition, 'his' – pronoun, 'leg' – common noun. Eight different types.)

OPTICAL ILLUSIONS

———✦———

OPTICAL ILLUSIONS ARE something that tricks the eye or the mind. As well as being great fun, some of them give an insight into how the eye works. Here are some of the different types that will show whether you really can believe your eyes – or not.

Stare at the dot in the picture for twenty seconds. Now look at a white piece of paper. For an instant, you will see a famous lady, painted by Leonardo da Vinci.

This works because your retina (the surface at the back of the eyeball) retains images, especially ones with high contrast or brightness. Effectively, they're burned in, but it's only temporary. That's why staring at a lightbulb will resulting a green light in your vision even after you have looked away.

Your retina has a layer of light receptive cells, but it only covers 72% of the surface. The rest is the optic nerve that sends the signals to your brain. As a result, both your eyes contain a 'blind spot' that can be revealed.

Close your left eye and move the page so that the cross is in front of your right eye. Stare at the cross and hold the book at arm's length, moving it slowly towards you. At some point, the dot will vanish as it moves into the blind spot.

Your brain works by learning patterns, a constantly evolving mass of experience that works as a short-cut when you see a new object. Because of this, it can be fooled. Are you looking at circles within circles here, or a spiral? Your brain will see clues that make it believe it's a spiral, but something doesn't quite fit.

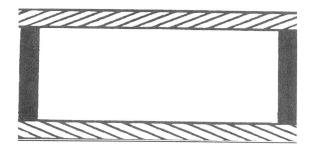

Are the two striped bars above closer on the right than the left? Measure and find out.

Sometimes, your brain just can't decide what it is looking at. In the image below, is this a block with a bit cut out, or with a piece stuck on?

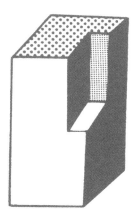

Here's one that involves fooling the brain into seeing movement.

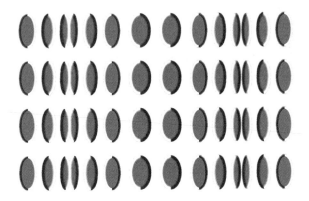

As well as these, there are thousands of well-known optical illusions. They are interesting in part because they challenge our belief that what we see is real.

Our bodies are wonderfully complex structures that carry our brains, held in bone and balanced on a spine. From that high viewpoint, we judge the world through senses that are not as reliable as we think.

The work of M.C. Escher is well worth a look if you want to stretch your brain a little.

THE LAWS OF RUGBY UNION AND RUGBY LEAGUE

—※—

A PUPIL OF RUGBY SCHOOL, William Webb Ellis, is credited as the first player to pick up a football and run with it – inventing the game of 'Rugby Football' in 1823. The trophy competed for at the Rugby Union World Cup is named in his honour, as is Ellis Stadium in Johannesburg.

The modern game still has two distinct codes – Rugby Union and Rugby League. The most obvious difference at first glance is that Rugby Union has fifteen players and Rugby League has only thirteen. Rugby Union was played first, with Rugby League splitting off after disagreements over payments in the late nineteenth century. Union matches were originally for amateurs only and a player who had played professional Rugby League was, until recently, banned from ever playing Rugby Union.

In 1995, the International Rugby Board removed all restrictions on Union games, allowing players to be paid as they are in other sports at the top level. However, the games themselves are still different in a number of ways. The Six Nations Championship (between Italy, France, Scotland, Wales, England and Ireland) and the Rugby World Cup are both played to Union rules, though there is also a Rugby League World Cup

RUGBY UNION SHIRT NUMBERS

	No.	Position
FORWARDS	1.	Loosehead prop
	2.	Hooker
	3.	Tighthead prop
	4.	Second row (lock)
	5.	Second row (lock)
	6.	Blindside flanker
	7.	Openside flanker
	8.	Number 8
BACKS	9.	Scrum-half
	10.	Fly-half (outside half)
	11.	Left wing
	12.	Inside centre
	13.	Outside centre
	14.	Right wing
	15.	Full-back

Two teams of fifteen players compete for two halves of forty minutes on a grass pitch to gain points through tries, conversions, drop goals or penalties. A referee is in charge of the game and is supported by two flag-carrying 'touch judges' on the touchlines. The maximum distance between the H-shaped posts at each end is 110 yards (100 m), though behind each post there is an 'in-goal area', ending in a 'dead-ball line' that is between 11–24 yards (10–22mm) long.

Kick-off. Which team kicks off is decided by the referee tossing a coin. The successful team drop-kicks the ball from the centre of the halfway line. (A drop kick is when the ball is kicked after bouncing on the ground – usually at the moment of impact with the ground.) It must travel at least ten metres or the opposing team can restart with a scrum on the halfway line or ask for the kick to be taken again. In the same way, after every try and every success-ful penalty kick or drop goal, the team that didn't score restarts play with a drop kick from the halfway line.

Rucks. If a player is holding the ball, he can be tackled, ideally around the lower legs. Tackles around the neck are considered dangerous play and not permitted. Once he is down, he has to release the ball immediately. His own team want to keep possession, while the opposing team want to gain it. Both teams are allowed to pile in from behind the ball, but not from the side without earning a penalty, and players must bind onto a team-mate. If the ball comes free, it can be picked up and play can continue. A ruck always involves the ball being on the ground. It cannot be handled and must be 'rucked' backwards with the feet.

Mauls. A maul resembles a fast-moving, fast-forming scrum, with the ball still being held (and so not touching the ground). They form when a tackle holds up the ball rather than slamming the opposing player into the ground. As with rucks, players can only come charging in from behind the ball. A maul can collapse as it moves forward, in which case a scrum or penalty will usually be given, depending on circumstances.

Scrums. A scrum is a way of restarting play after a number of different infringements. For example, players are only allowed to pass backwards. Even if the ball is accidentally knocked forward, the referee will stop play and award a scrum to the other team. It is a huge advantage to be the team putting the ball into the scrum. Scrums are also given when the ball doesn't come out quickly from a ruck or a maul.

Unlike a ruck or maul, only the eight forwards take part in a scrum – usually the heaviest, toughest men in the team, though not always. The hooker, two props, two second rows, two flankers and the number 8 all link arms in a 3-4-1 formation, ready to lock heads with the opposing forwards. The hooker in the middle of the front row is the most important player in the scrum – it's their job to hook the ball out backwards for the scrum-half.

Offside takes many forms in rugby, but in open play it occurs when a player is in front of a team-mate with the ball. It's all to do with the fact that they must not obstruct opposing players – whereas in American Football, 'running interference' is actually a crucial part of the game.

Finally, the **line-out** is a way of restarting the game when the ball passes out of play on the touch lines. Whichever team didn't send it out of play throws the ball to a line of between two and eight players from each team. Whichever team throws the ball also chooses the number in the line-out and tends to have the advantage. The ball is thrown straight down the middle, and the throwing team usually wins the line-out because, by using secret calls, they know the likely length of the throw.

A **try** brings five points and is awarded when the ball is grounded in the opponents' in-goal area. The try must then be 'converted' for another two points. A **conversion** is a kick taken from a point in line with where the try was touched down. The ball must pass above the crossbar and through the top uprights of the H. The easiest conversions are directly in front of the posts, which is why you will sometimes see players reach the opponents' try line and then run along to touch the ball down under the goalposts.

If a **penalty** is awarded when the team is in range of the posts, a penalty kick will usually be attempted – for three points. As with conversions, this is normally a stationary place kick. A **drop goal** is a ball in normal play that is drop-kicked from the hands between the uprights for three points. Penalty kicks and drop goals have come to be an important part of the modern game.

RUGBY LEAGUE SHIRT NUMBERS

	No.	Position
BACKS	1.	Full-back
	2.	Wing
	3.	Centre
	4.	Centre
	5.	Wing
	6.	Stand-off
	7.	Scrum-half
FORWARDS	8.	Prop forward
	9.	Hooker
	10.	Prop forward
	11.	Second row
	12.	Second row
	13.	Loose forward

In Rugby League, a try is worth four points, though the conversion is still worth two. A penalty goal is also worth two and a field or drop goal just one point. Apart from scoring, the two most important differences are 'play-the-ball' and the 'six-tackle rule'.

Play-the-ball is one of the things that makes Rugby League a fast-moving, exciting game to watch, with fewer stop-pages than Rugby Union games. When a player is tackled, all opposing players but two must retreat ten metres from the tackled player. The two markers remain in front as he places the ball on the ground and rolls it backwards with his foot to the player behind them. It is also acceptable for the player to roll the ball back, step over it and pick it up himself.

The six-tackle rule further differentiates the two kinds of rugby. In League, there can only be five of these tackles where the ball is passed back into play. If a sixth tackle occurs, the ball is handed over to the opponents, so it's usually kicked high as it comes back into play after the fifth tackle, gaining ground in the process. Ideally, of course, the set of six would gain enough ground to go for a try or a drop goal.

Both kinds of rugby can be exciting to watch and the sport has not suffered from some of the crowd troubles that have affected football in recent years. A single chapter cannot cover every aspect of a complex game, unfortunately. For those who wish to go further, there are local clubs all over the country. A definitive collection of Union rules is published by the International Rugby Board: *The Laws of the Game of Rugby Union* (ISBN 0954093909). Alternatively, the Rugby Football League publish a 52-page booklet: *Rugby Football League: Laws of the Game and Notes on the Laws* (ISBN 0902039032).

GIRLS

You MAY ALREADY have noticed that girls are quite different from you. By this, we do not mean the physical differences, more the fact that they remain unimpressed by your mastery of a game involving wizards, or your understanding of Morse Code. Some will be impressed, of course, but as a general rule, girls do not get quite as excited by the use of urine as a secret ink as boys do.

We thought long and hard about what advice could possibly be suitable. It is an inescapable fact that boys spend a great deal of their lives thinking and dreaming about girls, so the subject should be mentioned here – as delicately as possible.

ADVICE ABOUT GIRLS

1. It is important to listen. Human beings are often very self-centred and like to talk about themselves. In addition, it's an easy subject if someone is nervous. It is good advice to listen closely – unless she has also been given this advice, in which case an uneasy silence could develop, like two owls sitting together.

2. Be careful with humour. It is very common for boys to try to impress girls with a string of jokes, each one

more desperate than the last. One joke, perhaps, and then a long silence while she talks about herself ...

3. When you are older, flowers really do work – women love them. When you are young, however, there is a ghastly sense of being awkward rather than romantic – and she will guess your mother bought them.

4. Valentine's Day cards. Do not put your name on them. The whole point is the excitement a girl feels, wondering who finds her attractive. If it says 'From Brian' on it, the magic isn't really there. This is actually quite a nice thing to do to someone you don't think will get a card. If you do this, it is even more important that you never say, 'I sent you one because I thought you wouldn't get any.' Keep the cards simple. You do not want one with padding of any kind.

5. Avoid being vulgar. Excitable bouts of wind-breaking will not endear you to a girl, just to pick one example.

6. Play sport of some kind. It doesn't matter what it is, as long as it replaces the corpse-like pallor of the computer programmer with a ruddy glow. Honestly, this is more important than you know.

7. If you see a girl in need of help – unable to lift something, for example – do not taunt her. Approach the object and greet her with a cheerful smile, whilst sur-

reptitiously testing the weight of the object. If you find you can lift it, go ahead. If you can't, try sitting on it and engaging her in conversation.

8. Finally, make sure you are well-scrubbed, your nails are clean and your hair is washed. Remember that girls are as nervous around you as you are around them, if you can imagine such a thing. They think and act rather differently to you, but without them, life would be one long rugby locker room. Treat them with respect.

THE PATRON SAINTS OF BRITAIN

———✦———

THE UNITED KINGDOM is made up of four main countries: England, Scotland, Wales and Northern Ireland. Each country has its own flag and the United Kingdom has the Union Flag, first created in 1606. It is a combination of the cross of St Andrew for Scotland, the cross of St George for England and the cross of St Patrick for Ireland. Wales was joined with England in 1536 as a principality rather than a separate kingdom and is therefore also represented by the cross of St George.

The story of the patron saint of England slaying a monstrous dragon is known by all schoolchildren, but whether he existed at all and how he became the English patron saint is still a bit of a mystery. One light-hearted story suggests that St George made a huge fortune selling bacon to the Roman Army and that's why the English, 'a nation of shopkeepers', adopted him as a saint.

The man who was canonised as St George was a Roman soldier who served in England. One of the few solid facts around this enigmatic man is that he was killed in AD 303, during the persecution of Christians by the Emperor Diocletian. The Archbishop of Genoa compiled a collection of the lives of the saints and tells us that after St George had slain the dragon, he gave up his knightly wealth and preached about Jesus Christ until he saw Diocletian's cruelty. He scolded the emperor and was tortured and beheaded for speaking out.

Edward the Confessor was the patron saint of England until the Plantagenets adopted St George in 1348. The Order of the Garter was created by Edward III. He and his son (also Edward, known as the Black Prince) were the first members of what is one of the world's oldest surviving orders of chivalry. A gold collar is part of the insignia, carrying a representation of George and the dragon known as 'the Great George'. When not wearing the Great George, Knights of the Garter are required to wear 'the lesser George', a small image of the saint.

The annual Order of the Garter service takes place in St George's Chapel at Windsor, built by Edward III in the same year as the founding of the order. A heart, supposedly St George's, rests there as a holy relic. Interestingly, there were foreign knights in the order almost from the beginning. Edward III and his son had conquered areas of France, eventually capturing the King of France and holding him in London. As a result, Edward was Lord of Gascony, for example, and could accept the allegiance of French nobles. The tradition of 'stranger knights' has continued for centuries, with foreign kings and princes joining the order. That said, the German Kaiser had his membership cancelled when the First World War broke out.

St George's Day is celebrated on 23 April, when his red and white flag is flown from every Anglican church in England. He is also the patron saint of Portugal and Malta and even has his own country named after him, Georgia.

The life of David of Wales has its own elements of mystery. The primary source for information on his life comes from an eleventh-century Latin manuscript. David was not actually adopted as patron of Wales until the 1800s – another reason why he is not represented in the Union Flag.

He lived in the sixth century AD and is said to have been a son of the King of Cardiganshire in west Wales. He was deeply devout and must have been a man of great eloquence and charisma. He was a priest, a monk and eventually a bishop. He established churches and monasteries, went on pilgrimage to Jerusalem and, against his will, was made an archbishop after impressing other churchmen with his piety and the miracles that followed in his wake. More than once, spring water is said to have come from stone at his touch and he is credited with raising one young boy from the dead. When the crowd complained that they could not see him, the ground is reported to have risen under him until he was visible to all.

David settled in south-west Wales, founding a very strict religious community there. The monks were not allowed to use animals for labour, to give just one example, so that they had to plough the fields with their own strength alone. He himself drank only water and ate bread and herbs. He is said to have been tall and strong and the diet obviously suited him. He reached a very old age – some say over a hundred – and died in AD 589. In his last sermon, he urged parishioners to 'do the little things' – the small examples of kindness and decency that are so important in our lives. He was canonised (made a saint) in 1120. St David's Day of 1 March is a popular event in Wales and across Britain, marked by the wearing of daffodils, or leeks, Welsh national emblems.

3. St Patrick – 17 March

St Patrick was born around AD 385–7. The exact location is unknown, though he is generally supposed to have been Anglo-Roman. His parents were Romans living in Britain in the final days of empire.

When he was still very young, he was captured by sea raiders and taken to Ireland as a slave. He escaped while in his early twenties, making his way to the coast and finding sailors who returned him to Britain. There, he studied to become a priest and was later made a bishop.

He returned to Ireland as one of the first Christian missionaries and began a life of extraordinary energy and leadership. His first convert was a chieftain named Dichu who intended to kill the stranger on his shores. However, Dichu found he could not raise his arm in anger against Patrick and accepted the new faith he brought with him.

Like David in Wales, Patrick created monasteries and convents all over Ireland, making his base in Armagh in the north. He preached and taught constantly, building churches and converting whole areas. It was no easy task. Ireland was pagan and bloody when Patrick came. He struggled against ancient sun worship and dark statues of fertility gods like Crom-Cruach, whose followers sacrificed themselves and their children in his honour. Patrick cast down its statue and cursed it, an act of both faith and personal bravery. In far lighter vein, he is said to have banished all the snakes from Ireland. The proof of his effectiveness is the fact that there are no snakes in Ireland.

Miracles followed Patrick and he lit a fire of faith in Ireland that burns today. Perhaps the most famous example of his teaching is in the three-leafed clover known as a shamrock. Patrick used it to show how a trinity – father, son and holy spirit – could also be one, just as the three leaves were one shamrock. It has been Ireland's national symbol ever since. After years of living in poverty, travelling and enduring much suffering he died in AD 461, on 17 March. His life is celebrated on that day around the world wherever there are Irish gathered together.

4. St Andrew – 30 November

The Order of the Thistle is a form of knighthood restricted to the King or Queen and sixteen others. It was established by James II in 1687. It is also known as The Order of St Andrew.

Andrew has the distinction of being by far the oldest of our patron saints. He was the first of the original apostles, a fisherman in Galilee and brother to St Peter, the first Pope. Andrew is the apostle who introduced a boy with five loaves and two fishes to Jesus. Very little is known about his life after his involvement with Jesus, though he is said to have taken the new faith into Asia Minor (modern-day Turkey) and Greece. He was eventually crucified by the Romans for spreading the Christian faith.

His path to becoming Scotland's saint began when his

bones were moved from a simple tomb three hundred years after his death. The Roman emperor Constantine was a fervent Christian convert. He wanted the relics of one of the original apostles of Christ moved to his new eastern capital, Constantinople – now called Istanbul.

Andrew became the patron saint of Byzantium, the eastern Roman empire. There are a couple of tales as to how his bones found their way north. One is that a Greek monk had a dream where an angel told him to take them to the ends of the earth. He removed some of the bones and was shipwrecked off Scotland trying to fulfil his mission. They may also have been brought back by Acca, the bishop of Hexham, in the eighth century. A church was built to house them and in the twelfth century St Andrew's Cathedral was erected on the site. Sadly, the original Scottish bones have been lost, though Pope Paul VI sent relics of the saint to Scotland in 1969. They are displayed in St

Mary's Roman Catholic Cathedral in Edinburgh.

The Constantinople bones were taken to Amalfi. They remain today in the beautiful cathedral of St Andrew there, just a minute's walk from the sea.

LATIN PHRASES EVERY BOY SHOULD KNOW

THERE ARE HUNDREDS of thousands of Latin roots in English. If that wasn't enough, some Latin words have become so common they are often believed to be English! 'Agenda' (things to be done), 'alter ego' (other self), 'exit' (he/she leaves), 'verbatim' (word for word) and 'video' (I see) fall into that group. There is satisfaction in understanding your own language – and that includes its origins.

Latin phrases crop up in conversation as well as the law courts. It is still the gold standard of education, but be warned – showing off is not a suitable reason for learning this list.

The precision of Latin can be a pleasure, but the main reason for this chapter is cultural. The three pillars of British culture are the King James Bible, the complete works of Shakespeare – and Latin. If you know English, you should know a little Latin. What follows can only ever be a small sample of the whole.

Learn one a day, perhaps. After each phrase, you'll find a home-made phonetic pronunciation guide. Stressed syllables are in capitals (SCIssors, DINosaur.) For some, you'll find an example of it being used.

1. **Ad hoc** (ad-hok). Literally 'to this'. Improvised or made up. 'I wrote an ad hoc poem.'
2. **Ad hominem** (ad HOM-in-em). This is a below-the-belt, personal attack, rather than a reasoned response to an argument.
3. **Ad infinitum** (ad in-fin-EYE-tum). To infinity – carried on endlessly. 'And so on and so on, ad infinitum…'
4. **Anno Domini** (AN-no DOM-in-eye). In the year of our Lord. Example: 'This is the year of our lord, 1492 – when Columbus sailed the ocean blue.'
5. **Ante meridiem** (AN-tay Mer-ID-ee-em). Before noon – 4 a.m., for instance.
6. **Aqua vitae** (AK-wa VIT-eye). Water of life. Most often used to refer to whisky or brandy.
7. **Audio** (ORD-i-o). I hear. Romans would probably have pronounced this like Audi cars.
8. **Bona fides** (BONE-uh FIDE-eez). Bona Fides are credentials establishing good faith or honesty. Technically it is nominative singular, though it is usually heard with a plural verb these days, because it ends in 's'.

9. **Carpe diem** (CAR-pay DEE-em). Seize the day, or use your time.

10. **Cave canem** (CAV-ay CAN-em). Beware of the dog. Found preserved in a mosaic floor in Pompeii, to name one place.

11. **Circa** (SUR-ca). Around – approximately. Julius Caesar was born circa 100 BC.

12. **Cogito ergo sum** (COG-it-o ER-go sum). 'I think, therefore I am' – a famous conclusion form René Descartes, the French philosopher. He considered the statement to be the only defensible proof of existence. All else could be fantasy.

13. **Curriculum vitae** (cur-IC-you-lum VEET-eye). The course of life – or school and work history. Usually abbreviated to CV.

14. **Deus ex machina** (DAY-us ex MAK-in-a). Literally, a god out of a machine, as when Greek playwrights would have Zeus lowered on wires to solve story problems. It has come to mean poor storytelling, where some outside force makes it all end well.

15. **Dulce et decorum est pro patria mori** (DOOL-chay et de-COR-um est pro pat-ri-ya MORE-ee). 'It is sweet and fitting to die for your country.' A line from Horace. Later used ironically by Wilfred Owen in a World War I poem.

16. **Ergo** (UR-go). Therefore.

17. **Exempli gratia** (ex-EM-pli GRAR-ti-ya). For (the sake of) example – usually abbreviated to 'e.g.'

18. **Fiat lux!** (FEE-at lux). Let there be light.

19. **Habeas corpus** (HABE-e-as CORP-us). Literally 'You must have the body'. This has come to mean that a person cannot be held without trial – the 'body' must be brought before a court.

20. **Iacta alea est** (YACT-a Ali-ya est). The die is cast. Julius Caesar said this on the Rubicon river, when he was deciding to cross it. He meant 'It's done. The decision is made.'

21. **In camera** (in CAM-e-ra). In secret – not in the open. 'The meeting was held in camera.'

22. **In flagrante delicto** (in flag-RANT-ay de-LICT-o). In 'flaming crime' – caught red-handed, or in the act.

23. **Ipso facto** (IP-so FACT-o). By the fact itself. 'I have barred my house to you. Ipso facto, you are not coming in.'

24. **Magna cum laude** (MAG-na coom LOUD-ay). With great praise and honour. 'He graduated magna cum laude.'

25. **Modus operandi** (MODE-us op-er-AND-ee). Method of operation – a person's professional style of habits.

26. **Non compos mentis** (non COM-pos MEN-tis). Not of sound mind. Cracked.

27. **Non sequitur** (non SEK-wit-er). Does not follow – a broken argument. 'He never takes a bath. He must prefer cats to dogs.'

28. **Nota bene** (NO-ta BEN-ay). Note well. Usually abbreviated to 'n.b.'. Note that 'Id est' is also very common and means 'that is'. 'Id est' is usually abbreviated to 'i.e'.

29. **Paterfamilias** (PAT-er-fam-IL-i-as). Father of the family – paternal figure.

30. **Persona non Grata** (Per-SONE-a non GRART-a). An unwelcome person.

31. **Post meridiem** (POST me-RID-ee-em). After noon – usually abbreviated to 'p.m.'.

32. **Post mortem** (post MOR-tem). After death. Usually taken to mean investigative surgery to determine cause of death.

33. **Postscriptum** (post-SCRIP-tum). Literally 'thing having been written afterwards'– usually abbreviated to 'p.s.'.

34. **Quis custodiet ipsos custodes?** (kwis cus-TOAD-ee-yet IP-soss cus-TOAD-ez). Who guards the guards?

35. **Quod erat demonstrandum** (kwod e-rat dem-on-STRAN-dum). Which was to be demonstrated. Usually written as QED at the end of arguments.

36. **Quo vadis?** (kwo VAD-is). Where are you going?

37. **Requiescat in pace** (rek-wi-ES-cat in par-kay). 'May he or she rest in peace' – usually abbreviated to RIP.

38. **Semper fidelis** (SEMP-er fid-EL-is). Always faithful. The motto of the United States Marines Corps. The motto of the Royal Air Force is 'Per ardua ad astra' – through difficulties to the stars. The Royal Marines motto is 'Per mare per terram' – by sea, by land.

39. **Senatus Populusque Romanus** (sen-AH-tus pop-yool-US-kway rome-ARN-us). The senate and the people of Rome. Imperial legions carried SPQR on their banners. Oddly enough, it is still to be found on drain-hole

covers in modern Rome.

40. **Status quo** (state-us kwo). 'The state in which things are.' The existing state of affairs. Example: 'It is crucial to maintain the status quo.'

41. **Stet** (stet). Let it stand. Leave it alone. Often used in manuscripts, to indicate that no editing change is necessary.

42. **Sub rosa** (sub ROSE-a). Under the rose – secret. From the custom of placing a rose over a doorframe to indicate what was said inside was not to be repeated.

43. **Tabula rasa** (TAB-yool-a RAR-sa). Literally a 'scraped tablet'. Blank slate. A state of innocence.

44. **Terra firma** (TER-a FIRM-a). Solid ground.

45. **Terra incognita** (TER-a in-cog-NIT-a). Land unknown. Used on old maps to show the bits as yet unexplored.

46. **Vade retro satana!** (VAR-day RET-ro sa-TARN-a). Get behind me, Satan. This is an order to crush desires or temptations to sin.

47. **Veni, vidi, vici** (WAYN-ee WEED-ee WEEK-ee). I came, I saw, I conquered. Said by Julius Caesar after a rebellion in Greece that he defeated in one afternoon.

48. **Versus** (VER-sus). Against – usually abbreviated to 'v' or 'vs.'

49. **Veto** (VEE-tow). I forbid. Another one so commonly used as to appear English.

50. **Vox populi** (vox POP-yool-ee). Voice of the people. Often abbreviated to a 'Vox Pop' – a short interview on the street.

There are only seven kinds of Roman numerals. These are: I, V, X, L, C, D and M. (1, 5, 10, 50, 100, 500 and 1000.) From just those seven, all other numbers can be made. The only difficulty comes in recognising that some numbers, like four and nine, are made by IV and IX – one less than five, one less than ten. This pattern is used all through Roman numerals, so nine hundred and ninety-nine will be IM. That's it. Spend ten minutes on this page and then go and read any gravestone you wish.

I II III IV V VI VII VIII IX X **(1–10)**

XI XII XIII XIV XV XVI XVII XVIII XIX XX **(11–20)**

XXX **(30)**   XL **(40)**   L **(50)**   LX **(60)**   LXX **(70)**

LXXX **(80)**   XC **(90)**   C **(100)**

The year 1924, for example, would be represented as MDCCCCXXIV.

FAMOUS BATTLES – PART ONE

⟨※⟩

IN THE MAIN, history springs from both noble and petty sources – from jealousy and murder as much as the dreams of great men and women. As well as being formed in new laws and sweeping cultural movements, history is made on the battlefield, with entire futures hanging on the outcome. You will find further study of these examples both enlightening and rewarding. Each is an extraordinary story in itself. Each had repercussions that helped to change the world.

1. Thermopylae – 480 BC

Darius the Great ruled the Persian lands known today as Iran and Iraq, pursuing an aggressive policy of expansion. He sent his heralds to Greek cities to demand submission. Many accepted, though Athens executed their herald and Sparta threw theirs down a well. War followed and Darius' ambitions came to an abrupt end when he was beaten at the Battle of Marathon in Greece. Although he planned another great invasion, his death prevented his return. It would fall to his son, Xerxes, to invade northern Greece with a vast army of more than two million in the spring of 480 bc.

The Persian fleet had already won control of the sea and the Greeks could not hold the north against such a vast host. Instead, they chose to defend the pass at Ther-

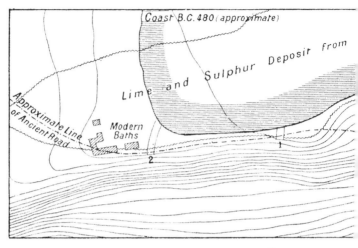

COAST AT MIDDLE GATE OF THERMOPYLÆ IN 480.
1, 2, 3, mark the three positions of the defenders of the Pass.
Scale, 8″ to 1 mile.

mopylae in the south. Here, the way through the mountains was a tiny path only fourteen feet wide at its narrowest point. Thermopylae means 'Hot Gates', named after thermal springs in the area.

The Spartan king, Leonidas, took his personal guard of three hundred Spartans and about 7,000 other foot soldiers and archers to the pass. Of all the Greek leaders, he alone seemed to understand the desperate importance of resisting the enemy horde. When he reached the pass, his men rebuilt an ancient wall and 6,000 of them waited at the middle gate, the other thousand guarding a mountain

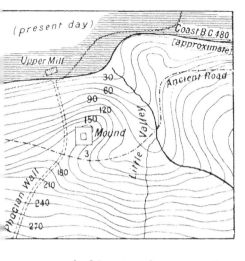

(present day)

Coast BC 480
(approximate)

Upper Mill

Ancient Road

30
60
90
120
150

Mound

Little Valley

Phocian Wall

180
210
240
270

3

trail above. They did not expect to survive, but Spartans were trained to scorn fear and hardship from a young age. They prided themselves on being elite warriors. The Royal Guard were all fathers, allowed to attend the king only after they had contributed to the gene pool of Sparta. They revered courage above all else.

The Persian king sent scouts to investigate the pass. He was surprised to hear that the Spartans were limbering up and braiding their hair for battle. Unable to believe that such a small group would honestly wish to fight, he sent a warning to withdraw or be destroyed. They made him wait for four days without a reply. On the fifth, the Persian army attacked.

From the beginning, the fighting was brutal in such a confined space. The Spartans and the other Greeks fought for three solid days, throwing the Persians back again and again. Xerxes was forced to send in his 'Immortals' – his best warriors. The Spartans proved they were poorly named by killing large numbers of them. Two of Xerxes' brothers were also killed in the fighting.

In the end, Leonidas was betrayed by a Greek traitor. The man went to Xerxes and told him about a mountain track leading around the pass at Thermopylae. Leonidas had guarded one track, but for those who knew the area, there were others. Xerxes sent more of his Immortals to the secret path and they attacked at dawn. The other Greek soldiers were quickly routed, but Leonidas and the Spartans fought on.

When Leonidas finally fell, he had been cut off from the rest of the Spartans. A small group of the guard fought their way into the heaving mass, recovered his body and carried him to where the others were surrounded, fighting all the way. The Persians simply could not break their defence and finally Xerxes ordered them to be cut down with flight after flight of heavy arrows. He was so furious at the losses his army had suffered that he had Leonidas beheaded and his body nailed to a cross.

The Spartans went on to play a crucial part in the war against the Persians. Leonidas and his small guard had established an extraordinary reputation, and larger forces of Spartans struck terror into the Persians at later battles. They had seen what only 300 could do and no one wanted to face 10,000 or 20,000. The Greeks won classic sea battles at Salamis and Eurymedon, destroying the Persian fleet. Over the next eight years, they beat the Persian host on land with battles at Plataea and Mycale. They lost Athens twice to the enemy and saw it completely destroyed. Much of the war has been forgotten, but the battle at Thermopylae still inspires writers and readers today. When peace returned, the Spartans placed a stone lion at the Hot Gates to mark where Leonidas created a legend. The epitaph reads: 'Go tell the Spartans, Stranger passing by, that here, obedient to their laws, we lie'.

2. Cannae – 216 BC

When the Latini tribe consolidated their hold on southern Italy, they joined two settlements into a city named Rome on seven hills. In the centuries that followed, they continued to explore their lands and boundaries, north and south, eventually crossing into Sicily. There, they came face to face with an outpost of the ancient and sophisticated Carthaginian empire. It was a clash of force and culture that launched generations of bitter conflict in what have come to be known as the Punic Wars and the first real test of Rome.

The Battle of Cannae is famous in part because the Roman legions were utterly annihilated. This is a surprisingly uncommon event. History has many more examples of battles where the defeated enemy were allowed to leave the field, sometimes almost intact. Cannae was a complete destruction of an army in just one day. It was very nearly the death knell for Rome herself.

The Romans had actually won the First Punic War, which lasted for seventeen years (264–241 BC), but it had not been a crushing defeat for the Carthaginians. They had had a gifted general in Hamilcar Barca, who had brought southern Spain under the rule of Carthage. Yet it was his son Hannibal who would invade Italy from Spain, cross the Alps with elephants and threaten the very gates of Rome. He commanded Carthaginian forces for the Second Punic War (218–201 BC).

Cannae is in southern Italy, near the heel of the 'boot'. Hannibal had come south the previous year, after destroying Roman armies of 40,000 and 25,000. Rome was in real danger.

The senate appointed a Dictator, Fabius, who tried to wear Hannibal's forces down by cutting lines of supply. It was a successful policy, but unpopular in a vengeful city that wanted to see the enemy destroyed rather than starved to death. New consuls were elected: Gaius Terentius Varro and Lucius Aemilius Paullus. The senate mustered an army of 80,000 infantry and 6,000 cavalry over which the consuls assumed joint leadership.

Hannibal's army had very few actual Carthaginians. When he entered what is today northern Italy, his forces consisted of 20,000 infantry (from Africa and Spain) and 6,000 cavalry. He recruited more from Gallic tribes in the north, but he was always outnumbered. In fact, the Romans had every possible advantage.

The two armies met on 2 August 216 BC. Hannibal and his army approached along the bank of a river, so he could not easily be flanked. He left 8,000 men to protect his camp. His cavalry was placed on both flanks and his infantry took position in the centre.

Varro was in command on the Roman side that day. He

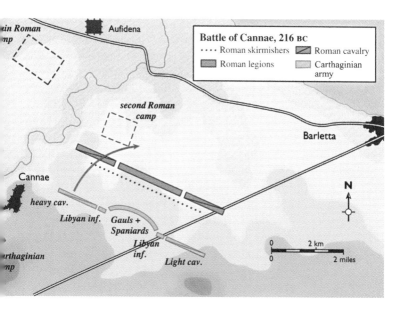

Aufidena

Main Roman
camp

second Roman
camp

Barletta

Cannae

heavy cav.

Libyan inf. · Gauls +
Spaniards
Libyan
inf.

Carthaginian
camp

Light cav.

N

0 — 2 km

0 — 2 miles

was not an imaginative leader and marched the Roman hammer straight at Hannibal's forces, attempting to smash them. Varro thought he had protected his wings from flanking manoeuvres with his own cavalry. In fact, Hannibal's horsemen were far superior. They crushed one Roman flank almost immediately, *circling behind* them to destroy the other wing as well. They then wreaked havoc on Roman lines from behind.

Varro pressed on, however, his front line pushing the forces of Carthage further and further back, like a bow bending. Hannibal's front line had become completely concave and Varro had no idea that it was part of the plan.

The Roman force marched further and further into the cup Hannibal had created for them. They believed they were winning.

Hannibal signalled for the wings to move and the cup began to close. Hannibal's cavalry completed the boxing-in of the Roman legions behind. They were so compressed they could hardly move and their numerical advantage had been completely cancelled out. More than 60,000 died over the next few hours as they were butchered, unable to escape. Hannibal lost 6,000 men.

One result of this battle was that the Romans learned from it. Three years later they had more than 200,000 men under arms and had renewed the struggle. There were successes and disasters on both sides, and Rome teetered on the brink of destruction until they appointed Publius Cornelius Scipio – known as Scipio Africanus. He had the vision and tactical skill to counter Hannibal. Though Rome was near bankruptcy and Italy was starving, the fortunes of Rome began to turn.

3. Julius Caesar's Invasions of Britain – 55 and 54 BC
Though neither invasion really came to anything, this has traditionally been the official starting point of recorded British history. In fact, Julius Caesar's own commentary is the *only* written source for some of the information that has survived today, such as the names of tribes around the south coast.

The Romans' first landing was on the beaches near Deal in Kent, having sailed from Gaul (France). The Britons (meaning 'painted ones', as they painted themselves blue) fought in the sea to prevent the landing, accompanied by huge dogs. Caesar's reference to the dogs makes the English mastiff the oldest recorded breed. The Roman force fought their way onto dry land and made a truce with the local inhabitants. It is important to remember that Britain was practically off the edge of maps at this time. The existence of 'foggy islands' or 'tin islands' somewhere past Gaul was considered a myth in some places. Caesar was overstretched and spent only three weeks in Britain before heading back across the Channel to Gaul.

The second landing in 54 BC was much better organised. Caesar returned with a fleet of 800 ships, five legions and 2,000 cavalry. As the Spanish Armada would discover fifteen hundred years later, the coast can be violent and a storm smashed a large number of his ships, scattering many more.

Caesar marched north, destroying the tribes who had gathered under their war chief, Cassivellaunus of the Catuvellauni. Cassivellanus was forced to sue for peace near modern St Albans. Caesar accepted and returned to Gaul. Events such as the great Gaul rebellion under Vercingetorix, a civil war in Rome, falling in love with the Egyptian queen Cleopatra and, finally, assassination would prevent him ever returning. The Romans did not come back to Britain until AD 43, under Emperor Claudius.

4. Hastings – 14 October 1066

This is one of the most famous dates in English history – the last successful invasion up to modern times. At first, after the Romans left, Britain was almost constantly invaded. First the Saxons proved bothersome, then just as everyone was settling down to being Anglo-Saxon, the Vikings arrived. The Danish king, Canute (sometimes written Cnut), created a small, stable empire early in the eleventh century, ruling England, Norway, Sweden and Denmark. He had taken the English throne from Ethelred the Unready and after Canute's death, his feckless sons lost it back to Ethelred's son Edward, known as the Confessor for his piety. He named Harold Godwinson as his heir, crowned King Harold in January 1066 – the last Anglo-Saxon king before the Normans arrived and spoiled it for everyone.

In fact, William of Normandy had probably been named heir by Edward the Confessor – as far back as 1051. William had also extracted a promise from Harold Godwinson to support that claim when Harold was shipwrecked off Normandy in 1064. In that sense, the 1066 landing was to protect his rightful throne, though that isn't the usual

view. We don't know the exact size of his army and estimates vary enormously. It was probably around 12,000
cavalry and 20,000 infantry.

In September, Harold was busy repulsing Norwegian
invasions. They had promised Harold's brother Tostig an
earldom for his aid. Harold marched north from London to
relieve York from a Norse army. He met them at Stamford
Bridge on 25 September, fighting for many hours. Of the
300 ships the Norwegians had brought over, only twenty-
four were needed for the survivors. Tostig was killed.
Stamford Bridge resulted in heavy casualties amongst
Harold's best soldiers, which was to prove of vital importance to the later battle at Hastings.

On 28 September, William of Normandy landed on the
Sussex coast. Harold heard of the landing by 2 October
and immediately marched 200 miles south – which his
army covered in less than five days. That is forty miles a
day with weapons and armour.

Harold rested his men in London from 6 to 11 October,
then marched to Hastings, covering fifty-six miles in forty-
eight hours. Again we have only estimates of the size of his
army, but it is believed to have been around 9,000 men. He
was badly outnumbered and only a third of his men were
first-rate troops. Still, it is difficult to see what else he
could have done.

Harold took position on Senlac Ridge, about eight miles
north-west of Hastings. On 14 October, the Norman army
advanced in three lines: archers, pikemen and cavalry.
William's archers fired first at too long a range, then fell

back through their own lines to allow the pikemen to reach the enemy. The second line stormed forward, but were battered back from the ridge by rocks, spears and furious hand-to-hand fighting.

William then led a charge up the ridge, but it too failed to penetrate. The Normans' left wing fell back and Harold's soldiers rushed forward to take advantage of their weakness. Harold's army was set to crush the invaders as a rumour went around that William had fallen.

William threw off his helmet and rode up and down his lines to let his men see he was alive. As well as being a splendid moment, his action does show the importance of charismatic leadership at this time, a tradition going back to Thermopylae and beyond. When they saw William, the Normans rallied and crushed their pursuers. Seeing how this strategy had worked to his advantage, William used the technique again. He staged a false cavalry panic and succeeded in drawing more of Harold's men from their position, his cavalry returning to cut them down. Yet most of Harold's men remained on the ridge and the battle was far from over.

Many assaults by infantry, archers and cavalry followed. Harold's forces were exhausted by mid-afternoon, but their courage had not faltered and they had sent back every attack against them. At that point, a chance arrow struck Harold in the eye, wounding him mortally. Morale plummeted and the English lines began to fail.

In terms of historical effect, this battle was the seed that would flower into the largest empire the world has ever known. Countries like Germany, Belgium and Italy have only existed as nation states in the last couple of centuries, but England has maintained her identity through a thousand years.

On Christmas Day 1066, in Westminster Abbey, William I was crowned King of England.

5. Crécy – 26 August 1346

This battle was part of the Hundred Years War. Fighting was not absolutely constant between 1337 and 1453, but there were eight major wars over the period between France and England. In addition, the French supported the Scots in their almost constant wars with England. It was a busy time and the period is fascinating and well worth a more detailed look than can be attempted here.

Edward III of England had declared himself King of France in 1338, a statement that did not go down well with the French King, Philip VI. In support of his claim, Edward invaded with a professional, experienced army of 3,000 heavy cavalry knights, 10,000 archers and 4,000 Welsh light infantry. An additional 3,000 squires, artisans and camp followers went with them. It is worth pointing out that the English longbow took more than a decade to learn to use well. It could not simply be picked up and shot, even after weeks of training. The strength required to fire an arrow through iron armour was only developed after years of building strength in the shoulders. It was necessary to start an archer at a young age to achieve the skill and power of those at Crécy.

Edward had failed to bring Philip to battle on two previous occasions. In 1346, he landed near Cherbourg and began a deliberate policy of the utter destruction of every French village and town he came to. In this way, Philip had to make an active response and his army marched against the English at the height of summer.

(The story of the early manoeuvres make excellent reading, especially Edward's crossing of the Somme river, made possible only by his archers and neat timing. The Osprey Military book *Crécy 1346: Triumph of the Black Prince* by David Nicolle is well worth buying.)

To counter the English longbows, Philip did have Italian crossbowmen, but they needed a protective wicker shield while they reloaded and these were still with the baggage train for this battle, leaving them vulnerable. Nevertheless, the French force outnumbered the English three to one, with 12,000 knights and men at arms, 6,000 crossbowmen, 17,000 light cavalry and as many as 25,000 foot conscripts. They were not well prepared when they came up against the English lines, however.

Philip's first action was to send his crossbowmen out to lay down fire. They moved forward and shot at 150 yards. Most of the bolts fell short and they advanced to fire again. This brought them inside the killing range of the English longbows and a storm of arrows struck them.

The French knights saw the Italian crossbowmen falter and assumed they had lost their nerve. The knights were so keen to attack that they rode down their own allies to get through to the front, killing many. Then they too were in range of the English longbowmen and the thundering cavalry charge was torn apart. Those who did make it to the English lines were met by unsmiling veterans carrying axes and swords.

Charge after wild charge followed and was destroyed by the archers and the grim men behind them. Edward's son, the Prince of Wales, played a part, though at one point his position was almost overrun by the maddened French. His father refused to send him aid, saying that he must win his spurs.

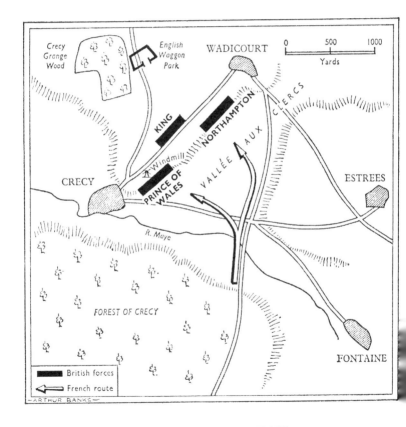

We know the exact number of French aristocracy killed, as careful records were kept: 1,542 knights died that day. The number of common dead is less certain – somewhere between ten and twenty thousand is the best estimate. In comparison, the English forces lost two hundred men, including two knights, forty men-at-arms and the rest from the Welsh infantry.

Crécy was a humiliation for the French king. It meant that Edward was able to go on to capture Calais on the north coast of France, which remained an English possession for almost two centuries.

Philip died in 1350, succeeded by his son, John, who was captured at the Battle of Poiters in 1356 by the Prince of Wales, then kept in London and held for a ransom of three million gold crowns. He never regained his father's throne.

This was not the last battle where cavalry played a part, far from it. After all, Winston Churchill took part in a cavalry charge in his youth some five hundred years later. Yet Crécy does mark the end of the *dominance* of cavalry. It showed the future was with infantry and projectile weapons, at least until the tank was invented.

THE LAWS OF CRICKET

BOWLING A MAN OUT or hitting a six is right up there with learning to drive, catching a fish, sailing a boat through a storm, shooting a rabbit, finishing a race, winning a fight and climbing a mountain. There are moments to be treasured in every life. Some of them can be found on the sports field. It is a myth that Wellington ever said that the Battle of Waterloo was 'won on the playing fields of Eton' – but the concept is revealing. Sport teaches discipline and aids fitness. There are few better ways of spending a summer than learning to play cricket. The game dates back as far as 1700, making it one of the oldest organised team sports in the world.

THE GAME

Cricket is a game for two teams of cleven. It is played on a pitch with wickets twenty-two yards apart – one 'chain' in imperial measurements. The wickets are made of three upright stumps with two horizontal wooden 'bails' resting on top. Each team scores runs by hitting the ball and running between the wickets, scoring one 'run' for each complete trip. Batsmen stay in to bat until they are 'out', which can happen in a variety of ways. When the tenth batsman is out, the team can no longer continue and the innings is over.

The cricket field or 'ground' itself is an oval shape and may range in size from 450 ft by 500 ft (137 × 150 m) to 525 ft by 550 ft (160 × 168 m). The wicket is in the middle of the oval and the boundary is usually marked with a rope.

Note the position of the umpires. There are two in a professional game. One stands behind the bowling end wicket, facing the batsman at the other end. The other stands square on to the batsman, watching the wicket from the side angle. (In international cricket, there is also a 'third umpire' off the field, who can

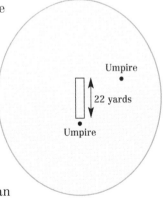

be requested by the on-field umpires to use video evidence to help with difficult decisions.)

In each team of eleven, there will be a captain, who is often a good batsman. There will also be a wicketkeeper who takes position directly behind the wicket when fielding. All players have to bat and field, but some specialise in bowling, some in batting and some are skilled in both – 'all-rounders'. A toss of a coin decides who bats first, then one team take up fielding positions and the other send out their first pair of batsmen – one at each wicket.

FIELDING POSITIONS

The captain and the bowler confer to decide the placing of the fielders. The bowler may find that a particular bats-man has a tendency to reach for dangerous shots on one side. The captain would then put more men in that area to catch a ball off the bat.

A lot of cricket terms, including fielding positions, refer to the 'leg' and 'off' sides. From the bowler's point of view, if the batsman is right-handed, the **leg side** is to the right and the **off side** is to the left. So the stump of the batsman's wicket on the right is called the leg stump. The other stump is called the off stump, and the middle stump? Well that's just called the middle stump. It's important to note that if the batsman is left-handed, then this is reversed. This is a good thing to get straight in your head early on.

Even at schoolboy level, you will still be expected to wear

pads, gloves and possibly a helmet when you bat, though probably not forearm and chest protectors. A groin cup, or 'box', is also a good idea. Cricket balls are solid cork wrapped in twine and leather. They are very hard and a good fast bowler can produce both fear and awe in batsmen.

The game goes forward in 'overs' – groups of six balls. The umpires usually keep six coins in their coats, moving one from one pocket to the other for each ball bowled. They change position at the end of the over. The bowler and fielders also move around and only the batsmen remain in the same places. In this way, both batsmen face the bowler. In theory, if single runs are scored, a batsman could find himself at the other end every time an over is called, but this evens out over long play. At anything greater than three schoolboys in a park, there is a bowler at each end bowling alternate overs.

BOWLING

The bowler bowls a ball of between $5\frac{1}{2}$ and $5\frac{3}{4}$ ounces (155–163 g). Its circumference must be between $8\frac{13}{16}$ and 9 inches (22.4–22.9 cm). Smaller versions are available for women's and junior cricket.

A bowler can bowl from either side of the wicket, as long as he mentions it to the umpire, who will then inform the batsman. The terms used are 'over' and 'around' the wicket. **Over the wicket** – the most common method – is when the bowler bowls from the side where his bowling arm is closest to the wicket. For a right-handed bowler, this would be the left side. **Around the wicket** is when the bowler bowls from the side where his bowling arm is furthest away from the wicket.

By the wicket there are several lines or 'creases'. The

line 4 ft (1.2 m) down the pitch is called the 'popping' or 'batting' crease. When bowling, the bowler's front foot can touch the popping crease, but must not step past it or a no ball is called by the umpire. There is another pair of creases at right angles to the popping crease – the 'return' creases. The bowler's trailing foot must end up between these two creases, or again a no ball can be called. The batsman can hit a no ball and can even be caught without being out – though he can be run out off a no ball. Even if he swings and

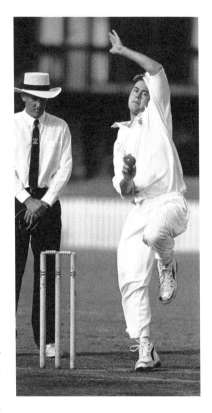

misses, one run is added to the team's score – though not to his personal total. 'No balls' are also called if the bowler chucks the ball rather than bowls it – that is, he throws it with a bent elbow.

A wide can be called if the ball is too high or far from the wicket for the batsman to reach using a normal cricket stroke. If the batsman, by moving, manages to hit a wide ball anyway, or gets close enough to hit it, the wide is not given after all. A wide is well worth leaving as it adds a run to the score – and another ball to the over. In theory, an over can go on for ever with wides and no balls.

Byes are runs scored when the ball whips straight past the batsman and wicketkeeper, touching nothing. Fast school-boy bowlers are particularly prone to this. The runs are added to the team score and not the batsman's. One reason to have a fielder at deep fine leg behind the wicket-keeper is to stop byes.

Leg byes are balls that whip through after striking some part of the batsman apart from his hands – an elbow, for example. This must not be deliberate on the part of the batsman. Leg byes are given only when the batsman tries for a shot. The runs are added to the team score, unless it's a glove deflection when they are added to the batsman's.

The bowler is allowed to rub the ball on his trousers to give it a shine, but not to use any external product. Running a hand through brilliantined hair and then rubbing the ball is strictly forbidden, as is picking at the seam to help the ball jump further on striking the ground. As with most sports, there are a thousand ways to cheat at cricket. It should not need to be said, but it is a matter of honour to play within the laws and within the spirit of the game.

The main different kinds of bowlers are fast bowlers, who rely primarily on speed, seamers, who aim to have the ball bounce on the seam, and spinners, who use either their wrists or their fingers to impart spin to the ball. Leg spinners normally bowl balls that turn from right to left – that is, from leg to off for a right-handed batsman. Off spinners bowl balls that turn from left to right – that is, from off to leg for a right-handed batsman. Bowlers will usually specialise in one of these areas, though a fast bowler will be quite capable of bowling with a bit of leg spin if the situation requires it.

The aim of bowling is obviously to take the wicket and send the batsman back to the pavilion. However, there are a number of ways to do this. It is extraordinarily satisfying to send a wicket tumbling through the air with a well-placed ball, but more wickets come from catches. For example, the bowler might place the ball with just a little spin so that the batsman tries a mighty blow and misjudges it, snicking a shot straight into the hands of the fielder. Not every bowl is aimed straight at the wicket. Bowlers are tactical thinkers. They tempt a batsman with an easy shot, perhaps, then lay another one in exactly the same place, but spinning the opposite way. The wicket falls. The only way to gain skill as a bowler is to practise in nets, learning how to be accurate.

LBW – leg before wicket. The batsman is not allowed to use his body or his pads to block the wicket. If a ball would have struck the stumps but was blocked, the bowler shouts 'How's that?' and the umpire raises a finger, indicating the man is out. Note that the point of impact has to be in a straight line between the wickets. If the batsman plays a shot, a ball outside that line cannot take an LBW, no matter how it swings in. You can see this rule applied occasionally when a batsman deliberately uses his pad to knock a leg-side ball away. The contact is outside the line and within the rules. LBW decisions are often a matter of controversy, but the umpire's decision is final.

A batsman can be bowled out, caught out, run out and given LBW. If he is caught out, the hand is allowed to touch the ground, but the ball must not. He can also be out if he breaks his own wicket, by accident or otherwise. A careless step back while batting has been the end of many a good innings. He is **run out** when the wicket is broken by the ball while he is between creases. At the highest level, this can come from a ball thrown by a fielder with extraordinary accuracy. At schoolboy level, it is usually thrown from a fielder to a wicketkeeper, who 'stumps' him, by knocking off the bails with the ball. Note that this can happen any time the ball is in play and a batsman steps outside his crease. If the batsman steps too far down the pitch to hit the ball and misses, there is a real danger that the wicketkeeper will take his wicket by catching the ball and stumping him.

UMPIRE SIGNALS

Out – raising one finger above the head.

---

4 scored – waving one arm from side to side at chest level.

---

6 scored – raising both arms above the head.

Wide – extending both arms to the sides.

No ball – extending one arm straight out to the side.

Bye – raising an open hand above the head.

Leg bye – touching a raised knee with a hand.

New ball – holding the ball above the head.

---

5 penalty runs to batting side score – repeated tapping of one shoulder with the opposite hand.

---

5 penalty runs to fielding side score – one hand placed on opposite shoulder.

The umpire will wait for the scorer to acknowledge the signal before play continues.

An umpire also has the power to send a player off the field for misconduct, effectively out. This can be for something as simple as deliberately obstructing an opposing player, disputing an umpire's decision, hitting the ball twice or even losing their temper and throwing the bat, which we once witnessed at a schoolboy match. It should be an indication of how despicable such behaviour is that the incident is still talked about a decade later. Team conduct is the responsibility of the team captains and in the first instance of poor behaviour, the umpire will have a word with the captain in question.

The only thing a batsman can do when he is called out is to walk. The best batsman do not even wait for the umpire to call it. They know when they are out and they leave the pitch without argument – though they may be internally furious with themselves.

BATTING

The best bats are famously made of willow. A bat should be no more than 3 ft 2 in (96.5 cm) in length and no more than 4¼ inches (10.8 cm) at its widest point. The handle is normally wrapped in rubber. It is crucial to have a firm grip and individual bats will depend on your height and build. Expert advice is needed when choosing a good bat. If you are left-handed, you will need to say so, as left-handed bats are fractionally different from right-handed ones.

Bats where the wood is covered are generally cheaper, as a poorer grade of willow is used. That said, they can still be good starter bats. Linseed oil should be used on the wood, with a small amount rubbed in and left for twenty-four hours. Be careful not to use more than a very small amount of oil. All bats need 'knocking in', a process of tapping the surface and edges with a mallet to compress the willow wood and make it better able to stand the impact of a hard ball.

You will also need a pair of pads, gloves, a box and a good stance. Stand with your legs slightly apart, with your weight on the balls of your feet, equally distributed. Point your front shoulder down the pitch at the other wicket. The knees should be slightly bent, the head still. The bat should rest on the ground near your back foot. The crucial thing is to be well balanced – able to move forward or backward easily. As the bowler runs in, you may find it helps balance to lift the bat towards third slip or gully – but bring it down *straight*.

A batsman's sole aim is to score runs. To do this, he must not lose his wicket. Cricket is not a slogger's game. A batsman who attempts to score four or six from every shot may manage it a few times in a row, but he will inevitably snick a ball and give someone an easy catch. A good batsman uses his judgement with every ball of every over. He watches the bowler carefully, observing how his hand moves to get an idea of the spin on the ball. He does not take his eyes off the ball as it leaves the bowler's hand.

There are seven main shots in batting: front-foot

defence, back-foot defence, a drive, a square cut, a pull, a sweep and a loft shot. Which one used will depend on how the ball moves and where it hits the ground. Note that reading about them is not a substitute for practising them! The first thing to remember is that you are less likely to get out if the ball is hit along the ground.

1. **Front-foot defence**. A good forward defensive stroke will smother a ball completely, stopping it almost dead. Step to where the ball pitches, angling the bat forward to knock the ball down. Played to balls pitched on a good length.

2. **Back-foot defence**. (Putting someone on the 'back foot' comes from this.) Used in response to fast balls pitching on a short length. When you see it is short, rock backwards, get the elbow high and knock the ball down with the angle of the bat. Keep the lower hand soft.

3. **Drives** – off-drive, square drive, cover drive, straight drive. The names come from the area of the pitch where you make the driving shot. Similar body position to the defensive shots, but the stroke is followed through rather than simply playing the ball into the ground. Front-  foot and back-foot drives begin as the defensive shots do, but the bat comes down fast and straight, swinging through. The front-foot drives are easier and less risky for inexperienced batsmen. The bat tends to end up above shoulder level.

4. A **square cut** is a shot to an off- stump short ball that pitches a little wide – usually a real wallop with a horizontal bat. The batsman's weight should come onto the back foot as

soon as you see it pitching short. Keep your head forward and roll your wrists to keep it down.

5. A **pull shot** is another response to a short ball. Weight on the back foot as it moves quickly towards off stump. The front foot moves out to the leg side, opening up the body. The bat comes across horizontally, with the face angled down into the ground to prevent an easy catch. Note that any shot where the bat is brought round horizontally is potentially dangerous and requires a good eye to hit it cleanly.

6. The **sweep shot**. This is played to a ball of good length, usually to a spin bowler. The front foot goes forward and the back foot goes down to kneel. This is another horizontal shot and must not be

employed against short-pitched balls, as they're likely to take your wicket – or your head off, one or the other.

7. The **loft**. Similar to a lob in tennis, in theory. It is crucial to keep your head down and still, with hands firm on the bat. Do not try this with an over-pitched delivery – only to short balls.

If a ball is pitched short and bounces high, a pull (or hook) shot or a loft could be used. Alternatively, you can just duck if you see it coming and react fast enough. No matter what you choose to do, however, never ever take your eye off the ball.

Part of the pleasure of batting is the partnership between the two players at either end. When scoring, partnerships are recorded as faithfully as individual scores, such is its importance to the game. Both partners call for runs, depending on who can see the ball. It is a responsibility that either builds or destroys trust in a very short time. A simple 'Yes!' or 'No!' or 'Wait!' are the usual calls from whichever batsman can see the ball. When you run, you must ground your bat at the far crease. At some point, we have all been run out after a bad call and had to leave the field through no real fault of our own. Calling is a matter of lightning judgement and remaining calm under pressure. Tempers and friendships rest on it.

If a batsman is injured, the umpires can allow a substitute to run and field for him. The substitute cannot bat, bowl or keep wicket, however.

Finally, a brief word on the ashes. On 29 August 1882, Australia beat England for the first time on English soil. A journalist, Reginald Shirley Brooks, wrote a mock obituary for English cricket that appeared in the *Sporting Times*.

> In affectionate remembrance of English cricket which died at the Oval on 29th August, 1882, deeply lamented by a large circle of sorrowing friends and acquaintances. RIP. NB – The body will be cremated and the ashes taken to Australia.

Arrangements had already been made for a return match and Ivo Bligh, later Lord Darnley, set out out three weeks later to 'recover the ashes'. A tiny urn containing the ashes of a bail was in fact presented to him in Australia after his team won two of the three test matches. After Darnley died in 1927, the urn was given to the MCC by his widow and can be viewed in the cricket museum at Lord's today.

A single chapter can never hope to cover every aspect of cricket. For the definitive answer to any question, buy *The Laws of Cricket* issued by Marylebone Cricket Club (ISBN: 1845790278).

UNDERSTANDING GRAMMAR – PART TWO

—✳—

GRAMMAR DOES BECOME more complicated when you look at sentences, as you might expect. However, there are in fact, only four *kinds* of simple sentences.

⌁ The Four Kinds of Sentence ⌁

1. **Imperative** (Command) – 'Get out of my office!'
2. **Interrogative** (Question) – 'Did you take my keys?'
3. **Exclamative** (Exclamation) – 'Fantastic!'
4. **Declarative** (Statement) – 'You are not my friend.'

As you see, a simple sentence can be very simple indeed. It needs a subject and a verb to be a sentence – so you need to know what a subject is.

Subject and Object –
⌁ nominative and accusative ⌁

The **subject** of a sentence is the person or thing acting on the verb. 'The man kicked the dog' has 'the man' as the subject. It does get a little harder to spot with the irregular verbs – 'John is sick' still has 'John' as the subject. The **nominative** form of words all have to do with the subject. This is crucial when it comes to pronouns, as the pronoun you use will depend on whether it is the subject or object in a sentence.

The **object** of the sentence is the person or thing on which the verb acts. 'The man kicked the dog' has 'the dog' as an object. The **accusative** forms of words all have to do with the object.

Before we go on to explaining nominative and accusative in more detail, you should know that Imperative or Exclamative sentences often have an invisible or implied subject. 'Get out!' does have a subject – the person doing the getting out, though the word isn't included. 'Fantastic!' as an exclamation implies 'That is ...' The verb is there in a sense, but not seen. All other sentences have a subject and a verb. Easy.

Nominative/Accusative Pronouns

When a pronoun is in the subject part of a sentence, we use nominative case pronouns. These are : *I*, *you*, *he*, *she*, *it*, *we*, *they*, *who* and *which*.

He went home.
    not
    'Him went home.'

He and I were good friends.

> *not*
>
> 'Him and me were good friends.'

She and Susan were going home.

> *not*
>
> 'Her and Susan were going home.'

We went to the park.

> *not*
>
> 'Us went to the park.'

Who struck Tim?

> *not*
>
> 'Whom struck Tim?'

In the above examples, the pronouns are all acting on the verbs, making it correct to use the nominative or subject form.

The accusative is the object part of a sentence. In the case of a pronoun, if it has the verb acting on it, we use *me, you, him, her, it, us, them, whom* and *which*.

Susan went with him.

> *not*
>
> 'Susan went with he.'

John loved her.

> *not*
>
> 'John loved she.'

David enjoyed playing chess with them.

> *not*
>
> '. . . chess with they.'

Why not come with us?
> *not*
>
> 'Why not come with we?'

We did not know whom to thank.
> *not*
>
> '...who to thank.'

Some of these examples are blindingly obvious. No one with the most casual knowledge of language would say 'John loved she'. However, 'who' and 'whom' cause problems still. It is worth giving those two words a small section of their own.

∽ Who and Whom ∽

Learn this: If the word in question is acting on a verb (subject/nominative), use 'who'. If it is being acted upon (object/accusative), use 'whom'. Be careful – this is tricky.

Examples:

1. *The man who walked home was hit by a bus.* Correct or incorrect? Well, the 'who' in question is doing the walking, so it is in the nominative form = accusative = correct. (You would not say 'Him was hit by a bus', but 'He was hit by a bus.')

2. *The man whom we saved was hit by a bus.* Correct or incorrect? This time, the man has been saved. The verb

is acting on him. He is not doing the saving, so it is in the object form = accusative = correct to use 'whom' here. (You would not say 'We saved he', but 'We saved him'.)

3. *He was walking with his mother, whom he adored.* Correct or incorrect? She is not doing the adoring. The 'who' or 'whom' in question is being acted upon by the verb and therefore should be in the object form = accusative = correct.

Finally, for the 'who' and 'whom' section, prepositions must be mentioned. Most examples of 'whom' are used when it is the object of a preposition. Note that it is still the accusative form. There is nothing new here, but this one gives a great deal of trouble. The form often comes as sentences are rearranged so as not to leave a preposition at the end. It has the added bonus of putting a key word at the end of the sentence, which works very well for emphasis.

1. *He was a man for whom I could not find respect.* If this had been written, 'He was a man I could not find respect for', it would have been wrong. 'For' is a preposition and you just don't end a sentence with them. Note that it could have been written 'He was a man I could not respect' – to avoid the problem. This is laziness, however. Learn it and use it.

2. *To Whom it may concern* – a formal opening in letters. Note that such a letter should be ended, *Yours faithfully*. If the letter begins with a name, *Dear David*, for example, it should end with *Yours sincerely*.

A final mention of pronouns in the accusative must be made. It should now be clear enough why it's 'between you and me' – the 'me' is in the accusative, acted on by the preposition 'between'. You would not say, 'He gave the car to I', which has 'to' as a preposition, or 'Come with I'. Similarly, you don't say, 'Between you and I'.

As You Now Know
⌁ Nominative and Accusative ⌁

For the record, **Genitive** has to do with possessive words: *mine*, *my*, *his*, *hers*, *ours* etc. Easy.

Dative is the term used to describe an indirect object. In the sentence 'Give me the ball', 'the ball' is the object, or accusative. However, 'me' is also in the accusative, as if the sentence had been written 'Give the ball to me.' The word 'me' is 'in the dative' – an indirect object.

Note that dative is of very little importance in English. In Latin, sentence word order is less important. 'The man bites the dog' can be written as 'The dog bites the man' – and only the endings will change. As a result, the word endings become crucial for understanding.

English has evolved a more rigid word order and so the dative, for example, has become less important. It's still satisfying to know it though and most modern English teachers can be made to glaze over with a question on this subject. That said, if you try it on a Latin teacher, you'll be there all day ...

The **Ablative** case is another one more relevant to the study of Latin than English. It involves words that indicate the agent or cause of an event, its manner and the instrument with which the action is done. The ablative case is likely to be used in sentences with the words 'from', 'in', 'by' and 'with' – prepositions. 'They proceeded *in silence*,' for example, shows the manner in which they proceeded. 'He was beaten *with sticks*,' shows how he was beaten. Those phrases are 'in the ablative'.

∽ Clauses and Phrases ∾

Simple sentences are not the whole story, of course. A complex sentence is one that has 'two or more clauses', but what is a clause?

The simplest working definition of a **clause** is that it has a subject and a verb and is part of a larger sentence. Sometimes the subject is understood, or implied, but the verb should always be there. The following example is a sentence with two clauses, joined by the conjunction 'so': 'I could not stand the heat, so I leaped out of the window.'

In a sense, clauses are mini-sentences, separated either by conjunctions or punctuation.

This sentence has four clauses: 'Despite expecting the voice, I jumped a foot in the air, smashed a vase and rendered my daughter speechless.'

'Despite expecting the voice' is a subordinate clause, separated by a comma from the rest. (Subordinate means lesser – a clause that could be dropped without destroying the sentence.) 'I jumped a foot in the air' is the second clause, 'smashed a vase' is the third, and 'rendered my daughter speechless' is the last. The final two are joined with the conjunction 'and'.

Note that 'smashed a vase' has the subject implied from the 'I' earlier on.

Subordinate clauses cannot stand on their own. Main clauses like 'I jumped a foot in the air' are complete sentences, but 'Despite expecting the voice,' is not. On its own, it would beg the question 'Despite expecting the voice…what?'

Phrases are groups of words that do not necessarily contain a verb and subject. Expressed simply, they are every other kind of word grouping that is not a clause or main sentence. A phrase can even be a single word.

The main kinds of phrase: Adjectival (works like an adjective); Adverbial (works like an adverb); Noun (works like a noun); Prepositional (works like a preposition); and Verb (works like…um, a verb). If you want to impress an English teacher, ask them if part of a sentence is using an adjectival or prepositional phrase.

Examples:

1. 'I lived *in France*.' 'in France' is a prepositional phrase, as it is a group of words indicating position.

2. 'I thought you wanted to leave *early tonight*' is an adverbial phrase, as 'early tonight' modifies the verb 'leave'.

3. 'It was an elephant *of extraordinary size*.' 'Of extraordinary size' is an adjectival phrase as it adds information to the noun 'elephant.'

4. '*The bearded men in the room* stood up and left.' This is a noun phrase – it's just a more complicated name for the men, using more than just one word.

5. A verb phrase is a group of words often containing the verb itself – an exception to the general rule that phrases won't have verbs. 'You *will be going* to the play!' has 'will be going' as a phrase of three words combining as the verb.

In contrast to complex sentences, 'compound' sentences have either multiple subjects: 'You and I are going to have a little chat', or multiple verbs: 'He choked and died.'

EXTRAORDINARY STORIES –
PART TWO

Admiral Lord Viscount Horatio Nelson (1758–1805)

HORATIO NELSON was born at the rectory of the village of Burnham Thorpe, in Norfolk.

He entered the Royal Navy at the age of twelve, in 1770, joining the *Raisonnable* as a midshipman. Despite famously beginning every voyage with seasickness, he would spend thirty of the next thirty-five years at sea.

After the *Raisonnable*, he served as midshipman on the *Triumph* and the *Seahorse*, travelling to the Caribbean and the Arctic. His next voyage was to India, where he picked up a bout of malaria and had to be sent home. It would leave him with recurrent partial paralysis for the rest of his life. Despite this setback to his health, he passed for Lieutenant on 9 April 1777, two years after the American War of Independence had begun.

In September 1778, Nelson was made first lieutenant of the *Bristol* and in the same year, France allied with American rebels against Britain. With Britain at war, Nelson was appointed commander of the sloop *Badger* in December and made captain at the astonishingly young age of twenty, in June 1779.

He served in the American war before returning to the Caribbean to enforce sanctions on the new American states. He interpreted the law rigidly, which earned him the dislike of both traders and local governors. However, attempts to have Nelson removed came to nothing after he petitioned the Admiralty and George III directly in defence of his actions. On the Island of Nevis, he met and married Frances (Fanny) Nisbet.

This first stage of Nelson's life could easily have set the pattern for the rest. His relationship with the Admiralty had suffered during his time in the Caribbean – and even the King was unhappy at Nelson's association with his disreputable son, Prince William Henry. For five years, Nelson was 'beached' – on half pay and unable to find himself a command. If war with revolutionary France had not come in 1792, he may well have remained in that state for the rest of his career.

In January 1793, he was appointed in command of the *Agamemnon* and sent out to the Mediterranean fleet under Lord Hood and then Admiral Hotham. At first, Nelson was not pleased to be given a 64-gun ship-of-the-line as he believed his seniority entitled him to command a 74. However, he was very impressed at the *Agamemnon*'s agile handling – in part the result of a complete refit and a new copper bottom.

The *Agamemnon* was one of fourteen ships sent to intercept a French convoy early in 1795. When the two fleets came within sight of each other, the French decided to withdraw, but two of them collided in the excitement. The *Ca Ira* came off worse from the impact and visibly lost speed.

Nelson saw his chance and attacked the 84-gun ship, giving her a whole broadside from close range, with each gun double shotted. He continued to pound the French ship for two hours, sweeping back and forth across her stern. At that point, Admiral Hotham signalled for Nelson to disengage, rather than lose him to French ships returning to save their stricken colleague. The incident went a long way to associate the name of Nelson with quick thinking and excellent seamanship.

Nelson was given the task of securing Corsica as a base for the Royal Navy. This too was a successful endeavour, though he was blinded in the right eye by a stone splinter from a parapet struck by an enemy shell. Despite this injury, he returned to duty the following day.

The Battle of Cape St Vincent (1797) involved fifteen British ships of the line defeating twenty-seven Spanish ships of similar power. As more and more Spanish vessels appeared on the horizon, Admiral Jervis told Captain Calder to stop counting them out loud, saying, 'Enough, sir, no more of that, the die is cast and if there are fifty sail I will go through them.'

The fleets met off the coast of Portugal as the Spanish ships were making a run for Cadiz. With a straight thrust, Admiral Jervis split the Spanish line, then ordered his ships to tack in succession (turn into the wind) to prevent the gap being closed. Nelson was last but two in the line and saw that the manoeuvre could not be completed fast enough to prevent the Spanish escaping. He made a decision to disobey orders and turn his ship, HMS *Captain*, into the gap. In doing so, he took fire from seven Spanish ships, including the largest in the world, the 130-gun *Santissima Trinidad*. Despite heavy damage, losing the wheel and part of his masts, he led a boarding party onto the *San Nicolas* and then immediately across her to the *San Josef*, entangled and damaged on the opposite side. Nelson's cry was 'Westminster Abbey or glorious victory!' and in this way, he captured two Spanish ships of the line. He took the surrender of the Spanish captains and remained on board, cheered by every British ship that passed. His extraordinary part in the battle was later humorously referred to as 'Nelson's patent bridge for boarding enemy vessels'.

Nelson had distinguished himself again, this time as commodore, with captains under him. Despite his seniority, he had taken a huge risk in 'interpreting' orders received from Admiral Jervis. If he had failed, he could well have been court-martialled, but the Spanish fleet was smashed: outsailed, outgunned, outfought. Jervis was generous in his praise.

Nelson's great friend Captain Cuthbert Collingwood was there, as was Thomas Hardy, not yet a captain, in the ship *Minerve*. HMS *Victory* was also present as the flagship of the Admiral. Nelson was knighted as a result of this success and promoted to rear-admiral.

In the same year, his right arm was shattered during a failed attempt to capture Spanish treasure ships in the Canary Islands. It was amputated without anaesthetic. The following year, in 1798, Nelson took his ship across the Mediterranean in pursuit of the French fleet that had landed Napoleon in Egypt. The Battle of the Nile is one of Nelson's most impressive and crucial actions.

The Battle of the Nile

Napoleon had taken control of Alexandria on 2 July 1798. He revered its founder, Alexander the Great, and it must have been a moment of special glory for him to be in that ancient place. His army pushed on to take Cairo by 24 July. Nelson was in Syracuse on the east coast of Sicily when he heard the news of the French fleet's whereabouts in Aboukir Bay off the western mouth of the Nile. He put to sea immediately and on 1 August, a British lookout sighted the French at anchor. The French fleet had landed guns to defend their anchorage and felt themselves secure. What was to follow would deny Napoleon his chance of an eastern empire and cripple him at sea. In a very real sense, the future of the world pivoted on one man at that moment. It is possible there would not have been a British Empire to resist the Nazi machine 150 years later if Nelson had lost in Egypt.

The French fleet consisted of four frigates and thirteen ships of the line, including Napoleon's own 120-gun flag-ship, the *Orient*. Under Admiral Brueys, they were anchored close to shore and were ready to fight at anchor, gaining the advantage of a steady firing platform. They had even dismounted cannon from the land side to fire out to sea.

In contrast, Nelson had thirteen ships of the line. He attacked as darkness fell, his ships cutting *between* the French fleet and the shore. The French were thrown into confusion. Their guns and crews were all on the wrong side for the action and Nelson's captains hammered the enemy unmercifully. Within twenty minutes, the first three French ships had been silenced and the first five surrendered by eight o'clock.

During the battle, Nelson was struck by flying iron, tearing free a flap of skin that blinded his one good eye for a time. Seeing him stunned and bleeding copiously, his officers led him below, believing he was dying. He too considered the possibility and prepared letters to be sent to his wife. He refused treatment ahead of his men, and by the time he was finally stitched, news came that the *Orient* was on fire. Nelson insisted on being helped up on deck once more.

The *Orient*'s magazine exploded around ten o'clock that evening, an explosion that could be heard thirteen miles away in Alexandria. The French Admiral Brueys was amongst the dead. Nelson sent his only undamaged boat to pick up survivors, though the battle would not finish until the afternoon of the following day.

Not a single British ship was lost and only 218 killed. The French losses are estimated at around 1,700, with 3,000 more taken as prisoners. Nelson was made a baron and became an English hero. The French fought on to the very end, but of the seventeen ships that had faced the British in the beginning, only four survived, withdrawn by Admiral Villeneuve, a man who had a part yet to play in Nelson's life.

By 1801, Lord Nelson sailed with the fleet to Copenhagen as second in command to Admiral Sir Hyde Parker. The fleet had been sent to Denmark to break the armed neutrality of the Baltic states. Nelson entered the action on board HMS *Elephant*, with Thomas Foley as Captain and Captain Thomas Hardy present as a volunteer. The British ships engaged the Danish fleet and both sides took terrible losses. Famously, Parker sent Nelson the signal to disengage. When it was brought to his attention, Nelson put his telescope to his blind eye and claimed he could not see it. From this, the expression 'turning a blind eye' entered the language.

Another interesting presence is that of Captain William Bligh at the battle, in command of the 50-gun *Glatton*. Following his acquittal at court martial over the mutiny on the *Bounty*, Bligh had resumed active service.

The Danes fought with great courage against the veteran British fleet, but eventually succumbed and accepted Nelson's offer of a truce to spare them further losses. An armistice was quickly arranged and signed. Nelson was made a viscount for the part he had played. His old commanding officer, John Jervis, now Earl St Vincent, was among many who complimented Parker and Nelson in the Houses of Parliament. It was Jervis who said of the chances of a French invasion, 'I do not say they cannot come. I only say they cannot come by sea.'

Nelson was one of the most famous men in England at this point. When he walked to his ship before Trafalgar, people knelt in the street. Others held up their children to catch a glimpse. The bulk of French ships were blockaded in Cadiz in the south-west of Spain and Brest, the most westerly point of France, with the prowling British fleet beating up and down the Atlantic off the coasts, waiting for them. The chance to end the sea threat once and for all would come in 1805, off the coast of Spain.

Trafalgar

At Trafalgar, Nelson was in command of the fleet, with Collingwood as second and the Earl of Northesk third. The battle was fought on 21 October 1805, ever after known as Trafalgar Day. Nelson commanded twenty-seven ships of the line against thirty-three of the French equivalent. However, his gun crews could fire at twice the rate of the French and the British shooting was more accurate. Courage, gunnery and seamanship would prove decisive, as they had throughout the war.

In August 1805, Napoleon had written to his admirals: 'Come into the Channel. Bring our united fleet and England is ours... all will be over and six centuries of shame and insult will be avenged.' He had 90,000 men along the coast of France, but did not have the ships to take them across the English Channel. In desperation, he ordered Villeneuve out from Cadiz to engage the enemy.

Admiral Villeneuve came out on 20 October, watched by British frigate captains who signalled their movements in relays out to the main British force. Nelson wanted Villeneuve's ships and at first merely maintained a parallel course southwards. Before the attack, Nelson arranged his fleet into two divisions. He led the first himself from the *Victory*, with Thomas Hardy as captain. Collingwood led the second division from the *Royal Sovereign*. Instead of sliding along the French line of ships, Nelson had decided to cut straight through it, as had proved so successful at Cape St Vincent. The French and Spanish fleet numbered thirty-three ships of the line, with 2,652 guns and 25,200 men. The British fleet had twenty-seven ships of the line, 2,178 guns and 17,076 men. The names of the British ships read like a litany of mythical and historical references: *Victory*, *Royal Sovereign*, *Britannia*, *Temeraire*, *Prince*, *Tonnant*, *Belleisle*, *Revenge*, *Mars*, *Neptune*,

Spartiate, *Defiance*, *Conqueror*, *Defence*, *Colossus*, *Leviathan*, *Achille*, *Bellerophon*, *Minotaur*, *Orion*, *Swift-sure*, *Polyphemus*, *Africa*, *Agamemnon*, *Dreadnought*, *Ajax* and *Thunderer*.

Before the fleets joined, Nelson made his will, asking that his mistress Emma Hamilton be well treated and that his daughter Horatia use only the name Nelson, so that his surname would be remembered. He was a devout man, as might be expected from the son of a Church of England rector. His diary records the prayer he wrote that morning, recorded for posterity.

> May the Great God, whom I worship, grant to my country and for the benefit of Europe in general a great and glorious victory, and may no misconduct in anyone tarnish it, and may humanity after victory be the predominant feature in the British Fleet. For myself individually, I commit my life to Him who has made me and may His blessing light upon my endeavours for serving my country faithfully. To Him I resign myself and the just cause which is entrusted me to defend. Amen, amen, amen.

As mentioned in the Naval Flag Codes chapter, Nelson intended to send the signal 'Nelson confides that every man will do his duty.' He accepted 'England' as a change and then 'expects', as it was in the code book as a single flag, and so would be quicker. The final signal was 'England expects that every man will do his duty', which caused his friend Captain Collingwood to say 'What *is* Nelson signalling about? We all know what we have to do.'

The first shot of the battle was fired at the *Royal Sovereign*, who raked her attacker, a Spanish three-decker named the *Santa Anna*. The British squadrons bore the French guns without being able to reply as they approached the wide enemy line, but at last they were in amongst them and the air screamed with shot. The *Victory* was attacked by five ships, but fought her way through with the *Temeraire* in support. Nelson and Hardy didn't move from the quarterdeck, though Hardy's shoe buckle was dented by a splinter. The air was filled with smoke to such a degree that they were practically blind. Nelson certainly did not see the sniper on the French ship *Redoutable* aiming at his distinctive uniform. Nelson was hit and Hardy held him as he collapsed.

Nelson was carried below, pausing only to order the tiller ropes of the *Victory* adjusted. He was bleeding internally and had a musket bullet lodged in his spine. He told the doctor that he had felt it break his back and knew he was dying. The chaplain came to him and Nelson reminded him he had left a will and that his daughter and mistress, Emma Hamilton, were to be looked after. It was a world removed from the chaos topside, with French ships being hammered and striking their colours to the British fleet. Nelson asked for his old friend Hardy to come down to him. Hardy was in the thick of commanding the *Victory* and could not leave command for another hour. When he did arrive, he was shocked to see Nelson's condition. Nelson asked Hardy to send his personal effects to Emma Hamilton.

Despite having lost more than a dozen ships of the line, a French attack on the *Victory* was under way and Hardy was called back on deck. The surgeon confirmed to Nelson that there was nothing he could do.

When Hardy returned an hour later, the battle was won. Nelson's captains and crews had carried the day. Nelson asked Hardy again and again to look after Lady Hamilton after his death. Then he said the famous words, 'Kiss me, Hardy', and Hardy kissed him on the cheek. Nelson murmured, 'Now I am satisfied. Thank God I have done my duty'. Hardy stooped and kissed him again on the forehead and Nelson called out, 'Who is that?' 'It is Hardy,' the captain replied. 'God bless you, Hardy.' Death did not come with great swiftness for Nelson and he continued to speak to those around him, mentioning again and again that Emma Hamilton and his daughter should be looked after.

It is an interesting point that having Hardy kiss him goodbye was never questioned until rather prim Victorians suggested he might have said 'kismet'. It is true that the words were almost unintelligible and that Nelson was only partly coherent from his wound. However, he was a man who inspired fanatical loyalty and love from his band of brothers. Hardy had been with him almost from the beginning and would have seen nothing wrong in kissing the great man farewell as he went where they could not follow at last.

His tomb is exactly under the centre point of St Paul's dome in London. The wooden coffin inside was made from the timbers of Napoleon's flagship, the *Orient*. Nelson actually had it with him on the Victory and kept it propped behind his desk.

To preserve his body, it was soaked in brandy and the coffin encased in lead. It lies in the crypt alongside Cuthbert Collingwood and other captains who fought on that day. Both men have monuments above ground and they share the crypt with another famous name from British history – Arthur Wellesley, Duke of Wellington.

THE TEN COMMANDMENTS

WHAT COMPILERS OF modern versions of the Bible sometimes fail to appreciate is that the language of the King James Version has a grandeur, even a power, that their versions simply lack. It is no hardship to 'walk through a dark valley'. On the other hand, 'the valley of the shadow of death' is a different matter. Frankly, the rhythm and poetry are part of the effect and not to be lightly cast aside. We can find no better example of this than the Ten Commandments themselves. Book of Exodus,Chapter 20, Verses 1–17:

And God spake all these words, saying, I am the Lord thy God, which have brought thee out of the land of Egypt, out of the house of bondage.

1 Thou shalt have no other gods before me.

2 Thou shalt not make unto thee any graven image, or any likeness of any thing that is in heaven above, or that is in the earth beneath, or that is in the water under the earth: thou shalt not bow down thyself to them, nor serve them: for I the Lord thy God am a jealous God, visiting the iniquity of the fathers upon the children unto the third and fourth generation of them that hate me; and shewing mercy unto thousands of them that love me, and keep my commandments.

3 Thou shalt not take the name of the Lord thy God in vain; for the Lord will not hold him guiltless that taketh his name in vain.

4 Remember the sabbath day, to keep it holy. Six days shalt thou labour, and do all thy work: but the seventh day is the sabbath of the Lord thy God: in it thou shalt not do any work, thou, nor thy son, nor thy daughter, thy manservant, nor thy maidservant, nor thy cattle, nor thy stranger that is within thy gates: for in six days the Lord made heaven and earth, the sea, and all that in them is, and rested the seventh day: wherefore the Lord blessed the sabbath day, and hallowed it.

5   *Honour thy father and thy mother: that thy days may be long upon the land which the Lord thy God giveth thee.*

6   *Thou shalt not kill.*

7   *Thou shalt not commit adultery.*

8   *Thou shalt not steal.*

9   *Thou shalt not bear false witness against thy neighbour.*

10   *Thou shalt not covet thy neighbour's house, thou shalt not covet thy neighbour's wife, nor his manservant, nor his maidservant, nor his ox, nor his ass, nor any thing that is thy neighbour's.*

Verses 18 and 19:

And all the people saw the thunderings, and the lightnings, and the noise of the trumpet, and the mountain smoking: and when the people saw it, they removed, and stood afar off. And they said unto Moses, Speak thou with us, and we will hear: but let not God speak with us, lest we die.

A BRIEF HISTORY OF ARTILLERY

The ability to strike an enemy from far away has always appealed to soldiers and generals alike. Bows have been found from as early as 7400 BC, preserved in a bog at Holmegaard, Denmark. They may go back as far as 20,000 BC. Though such weapons were powerful and accurate, there has always been a search for more destruction and greater range. A city cannot be battered into submission by archers, after all.

The Meare Heath yew bow from Somerset, England – dated to c. 2500 BC.

Archimedes is one of the most famous early inventors of artillery weapons. In the defence of Syracuse in 214 to 212 BC, he used bronze mirrors to focus the sun and burn enemy ships.

The truth of this story was doubted for a long time. In the early 1970s, a Greek scientist, Dr Ioannis Sakkas, employed sixty Greek sailors in an experiment to see whether it was possible. All the men carried large oblong mirrors and used them to focus the sun onto a wooden ship one hundred and sixty feet away. The ship caught fire almost immediately.

Archimedes was an extraordinary thinker, the Leonardo da Vinci of an earlier age. He invented a number of other artillery weapons to sink Roman galleys, or hammer them from the city walls. He was not alone, however. The Greeks developed knowledge of pulleys, water pumps, cranes, even a small steam engine. It was a period of extraordinary scientific advancement – all of which was useful in creating weapons of long-distance destruction.

Early weapons were based on the spring power of a bow arm, pulled back by muscle or by a ratchet, as in this picture. Understanding pulleys in particular means that a man can repeat an easy action over and over to move large forces very slowly. In other words, heavy weapons can be wound back with the use of a few simple principles.

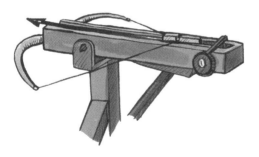

'Torsion' is the force gained by twisting. The Romans improved on Greek inventions, perfecting the use of ropes

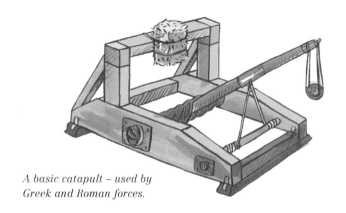

A basic catapult – used by Greek and Roman forces.

of woven horsehair and sinew as their 'spring'. The heavy Roman **'Onager'** was capable of sending a 100 lb (45 kg) rock up to 400 yards (365 m). An 'Onager' is Latin for a wild ass or donkey – with a fearsome kick. It is similar in

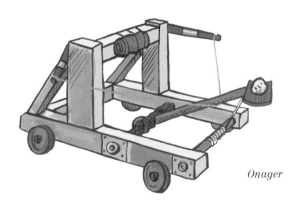

Onager

principle to the catapult, with a sling-like cup and a single torsion bar.

The **Ballista** was a Roman bolt or stone shooter. It used two torsion springs and had a range of up to 450 yards (411 m). The Romans also perfected a *repeating* ballista, invented by Dionysios of Alexandria. By simply winding a handle, the ratchet came back, an arrow dropped into place and was fired as soon as the winch reached its maximum point. This was the first machine gun – long before gunpowder.

Every Roman legion carried heavy onagers and thirty **Scorpion** bows – a smaller form of the weapon that could be carried on a single cart. Roman success in war depended on much more than discipline and a good gladius!

The last type of this sort of engine is a **Trebuchet**, powered by counter-weights. This form of artillery was able to launch heavier weights than any other kind. However, the enormous counterweight needed meant that they were practically immobile

Trebuchet

once set up and worked well only when battering city walls. They were in use throughout medieval times until the invention of cannon. Pulleys and ratchets were used to pull down the arm and load it. When released, the arm snapped forward and the second section whipped over at high speed.

Later, gunpowder and iron-foundry techniques combined to create smooth-bore cannons. Compared with early engines of war, these had a much longer range and were faster to load. Although China had gunpowder in the eleventh century, it was European countries that really exploited its use as a propellant in the thirteenth century. Roger Bacon, the English Archimedes, wrote down a formula for gunpowder in code in the thirteenth century. The combination of sulphur, charcoal and potassium nitrate, or saltpetre, would change the western world.

The picture below is of 'Mons Meg', a Flanders cannon cast before 1489 and currently kept in Edinburgh castle. It

fired a stone ball of 330 lb (150 kg) more than one and a half miles (2.4 km).

For the next six hundred years, cannons would remain essentially the same – smooth-bore muzzle loaders, lit by a taper or a flint-lock. Iron balls would be used instead of stone as they were easier to mass-produce and make uniform. Cast-iron barrels took the place of softer wrought iron. Cannons at sea could fire chain, or bar shot to destroy enemy rigging and clear the decks of boarding parties. In the basic principles, though, Nelson's cannons fired in the same way as those from the thirteenth century. As with most long-lasting technologies, if they weren't replaced, they were perfected.

Mortars and **Howitzers** were also perfected during the nineteenth century. A mortar fires at very high angles compared with a cannon, a howitzer between the two. Progress was fast and furious as a single clear advantage could mean the difference between winning a war and being invaded.

Rifling a barrel involves casting spiralling lines inside that make the ball or shell spin as it leaves, giving gyroscopic stability. Although it had long been in use for hand weapons, the practice was first applied to artillery around 1860. The new breed of artillery would be breech-loading, have reinforced barrels and be able to fire shells with astonishing accuracy.

The heaviest versions of these shell-firing weapons could be miles behind the lines, firing huge shells in a parabola (arc) at the enemy positions.

World War I British field piece, firing sixty-pound explosive shells

No chapter on artillery could be complete without a mention of **tanks**. From WWI onwards, these awesome machines have changed the face of warfare by allowing powerful artillery to be extremely mobile and well armoured.

In modern times artillery can take the form of inter-continental missiles, striking from hundreds or even thousands of miles away and with a greater force than anything else in this chapter. In a sense, artillery has reached its ultimate stage, where cities can be flattened without a single soldier entering the combat zone.

The twenty-first century – British Challenger 2 tank.

Shells can now be armoured in 'depleted uranium' – uranium with most of the radioactive isotopes removed. This is a heavy metal and hard enough to be ferociously efficient as an armour-piercing round. Though it is actually less radioactive than naturally occurring uranium, it is chemically toxic and should not be ingested. Dust and fragments from DU shells remain dangerous for a very long time.

We have come a long way from bow-based spring weapons. Until the invention of the machine gun, it was still possible to march into cannon fire and expect at least some of your army to reach the enemy. World War I changed that, the obsolete tactic going the way of the cavalry charge. It is difficult to predict the course of the future, with such immensely powerful weapons now available. Wars nowadays tend to be fought on a small scale, with major players being very careful to limit the destruction. In theory, Britain could have dropped nuclear weapons on Argentina during the Falklands War, or America on Iraq in the first or second Gulf War. Neither country took that step. Let us hope it does not happen in our lifetimes.

TIMERS AND TRIPWIRES

THESE ARE VERY simple to make – and deeply satisfying. For the timer, any wind-up alarm clock will do – preferably one with plastic hands. The idea is to use the clock to complete a circuit and turn on a light. You want the bulb to turn on in twenty minutes – to win a bet perhaps, or to frighten your little sister with the thought that a mad axe murderer is upstairs.

First, remove the plastic front of the clock. Tape wire to each hand, so that when one passes under the other, the bare ends will touch. It should be clear that a circuit can now be made with a time delay of however long it takes the minute hand to travel around and touch the hour hand.

Attach one of the wires to a positive battery terminal. Tape a torch bulb to the negative terminal and the end of the other wire to the end of the bulb. Test it a few times by touching the hands of the clock together. The bulb should light as the wires on the hands touch and complete the circuit.

Bear in mind that the hour hand will have moved by the time the minute hand comes round, so it's worth timing how long it takes for the bulb to light after setting the minute hand to, say, fifteen minutes before the hour. You can then terrify your young sister with the tale of Hamish McGee, the butcher of Margate.

TRIPWIRE

This is almost the same thing, in that it uses a battery circuit with a bulb linked to a switch – in this case a tripwire. With a long enough wire, the bulb can be lit some way from the actual trip switch for longer warning times.

You will need

- Clothes peg.
- Wine cork.
- Tin foil.
- Fishing line or string.
- Battery, bulb and insulated wire, as with the timer set-up.
- Adhesive tape.

Wrap foil around the ends of the wooden or plastic clothes peg. Attach your wires with tape to those foil ends, running both to exactly the same battery and bulb set-up as the alarm-clock switch above.

The important thing is to have a non-conducting item between the jaws of the clothes peg. We found a wine cork worked quite well. The wire itself must also be strong enough to pull the cork out – if it snaps, the bulb won't light. Fishing wire is perfect for this as it's strong and not that easy to see. It is also important to secure the clothes peg under a weight of some kind. Only the cork should move when the wire is pulled.

When the cork is pulled out, the jaws of the peg snap shut, touching the foil ends together, completing the circuit and lighting the bulb to alert you.

This works especially well in long grass, but its main disadvantage is that whoever trips the switch tends to know it has happened. Enemy soldiers would be put on the alert, knowing they were in trouble. Of course, in a real conflict, the wire would have pulled out the pin to a grenade.

PRESSURE PLATE

One way of setting up a trip warning without the person realising is with a pressure plate. Again, this relies on a simple bulb circuit, but this time the wires go to two pieces of cardboard held apart by a piece of squashable foam such as you might find in children's toy letters. A bit of sponge would also be perfect.

This time, tape foil squares over the bare ends of the wires on the inner surfaces of the cardboard and set up a simple bulb and battery circuit as before. With only light pressure from above, the two bits of cardboard come together, bringing the foil squares into contact. The circuit is made and the warning bulb comes on. Enjoy.

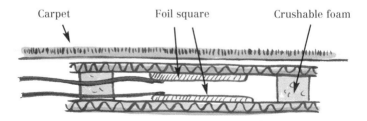

Carpet   Foil square   Crushable foam

THE ORIGIN OF WORDS

Eᴺɢʟɪꜱʜ ɪꜱ ᴀᴡᴀꜱʜ with interesting words and phrases; there are books the size of dictionaries chock-full of them. Here are twenty of our favourites – words and phrases with origins so interesting they should be part of general knowledge.

1. **Boycott.** Captain Charles Cunningham Boycott was a rent-collecting agent for an English landlord in Ireland in the nineteenth century. He was considered particularly harsh and locals refused to have anything to do with him. His name became a word meaning 'to ostracise'. It is used as a verb – 'to boycott', and as a noun – 'the boycott went well.'

2. **Halloween.** 'Hallow' is an old pronunciation of 'Holy', still sometimes found in the alternative version, 'All Hallows Eve'. The '-een' part is a common contraction of the word 'evening'. 'Halloween' means 'Holy evening' – also known as 'All Saints Eve'.

3. **Hooligan.** Almost certainly derived from the surname of an Irish family, 'Houlihan', whose name became synonymous with bad behaviour in the late nineteenth century.

4. **Quisling** (pronounced 'kwizling'). Norwegian Major Vidkun Quisling was a Norwegian politician who supported the Nazis in WWII. His name became synonymous with 'traitor'. He was shot for treason.

5. **Thug.** One of many Hindi words adopted into English (like 'pyjamas' and 'bungalow'). The 'Thugs' were a sect of robbers and murderers in India.

6. **Gerrymander** (pronounced 'jerry-manda'). A word derived from the surname of Elbridge Gerry, a US politician who in 1812 rearranged electoral districts to gain advantage for the Republican party. The new district was jokingly said to be shaped like a salamander and was depicted as such in a political cartoon that coined the term 'Gerry-mander.' His name has come to describe schemes to win elections dishonestly. His name began with a hard 'g', strangely enough, but the sound is soft on the word.

7. **Assassin.** The Arabic word 'hashshashin', meaning 'hashish eaters', was the name given to a violent Syrian sect in the Middle Ages. To create a murderous frenzy, they took hashish (cannabis) amidst chanting and dancing. The English word 'assassin' ultimately derives from this.

8. **Whisky.** From the Gaelic 'uisge beatha' (Ishka Ba-ha) – meaning 'water of life'. Other languages use very similar phrases – 'aquavit' for strong spirit in Scandinavia, 'eau-de-vie' for brandy in France, 'aqua vitae' in Latin. Vodka is Russian for 'little water'.

9. **Tawdry.** Meaning cheap and flashy. This word comes from the phrase 'Saint Audrey's lace'. St Audrey was a seventh century princess of East Anglia, who took religious orders. As a girl, she had been very fond of necklaces and when she succumbed to a throat disease, she felt it was punishment for her vanity. 'St Audrey's lace' or 'Tawdry lace' was tainted, or flawed, and came to mean flashy and poor quality.

10. **Cor blimey/Gorblimey.** Still heard around Britain, though mainly in London, sometimes contracted just to 'blimey'. This is a corruption of an old oath – 'God blind me.' In a similar way, 'Bloody' is thought to be a corruption of 'By our Lady' and one that has fallen out of use, 'Gadzooks!' is a form of 'God's hooks', making reference to the nails used in the crucifixion of Jesus. The Australian 'Strewth!' similarly, is a contraction of 'God's *Truth*.' Even oaths can have interesting histories.

11. **Exchequer.** In Norman England, money-counting tables were often covered in a chequered cloth. The practice was common enough for the table to become known as an 'eschequier', meaning 'chessboard', and the word transferred to English as 'exchequer', a word for the Treasury.

12. **Auspicious/augury.** In English, the words have to do with telling the future. 'It seemed an auspicious moment to apply for his job, when Jenkins fell down the well.' Both have their roots in the Roman practice of using the flight of birds to tell the future. An expert in this field was known as an 'auspex', derived from a combination of 'avis', meaning 'bird', and 'specere', 'to look'. These charlatans were literally 'lookers at birds', and the word survives two thousand years on.

13. **Chivalry.** The moral code of knights, who tended to ride horses. The name is derived from the French word for horse, 'cheval', which in turn comes from the Latin 'caballus'. 'Cavalier', meaning off-hand or 'too casual' (a cavalier attitude), also comes from the same root.

14. **Chortle.** A word invented by Lewis Carroll (writer of *Alice in Wonderland*) as a combination of 'chuckle'

and 'snort'. This type of combination is known as a 'portmanteau' word. He also invented the word 'portmanteau' to describe words of this type, like 'brunch', which is a combination of 'breakfast' and 'lunch'. Clever man.

15. **Conspire/Expire/Respire.** All these words have their origin in the Latin, 'spirare', to breathe. Conspirators breathe their plots together. A man who 'expires' has the breath go out of him. Respiration is breath.

16. **Denim.** This is one of many products linked to its place of origin. The hard-wearing cloth was created in Nimes, a southern French industrial town. It was known first as 'serge de Nimes' and then as 'de Nimes'.

17. **Laconic.** The region inhabited by the Spartans of ancient Greece was named Laconia. Philip of Macedonia (the father of Alexander the Great) sent this warning to the famous warriors of the city, to frighten them into obedience: 'If I enter Laconia with my army, I shall raze Sparta to the ground.' The Spartans replied with a single word : 'If.' 'Laconic' means terse, or to the point, in recognition of the Spartan style. The

word 'Spartan', meaning bare and without ornamentation, also comes from that warrior culture.

18. **Shambles.** Although it is now used to mean a chaotic scene, this word originally meant a slaughterhouse. In fact, reference to the fact that shambles were relocated after the great fire of London in 1666 can be found on Christopher Wren's Monument, (next to Monument tube station in London). The word origin goes even further back to Old English for a table, 'scamul', which is connected with the Latin for 'bench', 'scamnum'. Rows of these would form a meat market.

19. **Mob.** This word is simply a contraction of the Latin phrase, 'mobile vulgus' (MOB-e-lay, VULG-ous). 'Mobile' means fickle and 'Vulgus' means crowd.

20. **Quick.** In Old English, 'cwic' meant 'alive', a meaning we still see in 'quicksilver', another name for mercury, as the liquid metal seems almost to be a living silver. You may also have heard the phrase, 'the quick and the dead', meaning 'the living and the dead', or 'cut to the quick', meaning 'cut to the living flesh'. 'Quick-tempered' also retains some sense of the original sense, though the modern meaning is mainly to do with speed alone.

THE GREATEST PAPER PLANE
IN THE WORLD

IN THE 1950s, a secondary school headmaster found a
boy throwing paper planes from a high window. The
head was considering punishments when he noticed the
plane was still in the air, flying across the playground
below. The boy escaped a detention, but he did have to
pass on the design to the schoolmaster – who passed it on
to his own children. You will find more complicated
designs. You may be sold the idea that the best planes
require scissors and lessons in origami. This is nonsense.

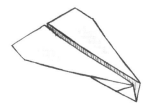 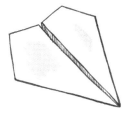

The plane on the right – the Harrier – is simple, fast and
can be made from a sheet of A4. It is the best long-distance glider you'll ever see – and with a tweak or two, the
best stunt plane. It has even won competitions. One was to
clear the entire road from a hotel balcony next to Windsor
Castle on New Year's Eve. Four other planes hit the tar-
mac – this one sailed clear across. The one on the left – the

Bulldog Dart – is a simple dart, a warm-up plane, if you like. It's a competent glider.

THE BULLDOG DART

1. Fold a sheet of A4 lengthways to get a centre line.
2. Fold two corners into the centre line, as in the picture.
3. Turn the paper over and fold those corners in half, as shown.

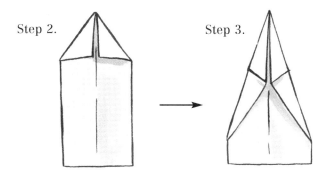

Step 2.   Step 3.

4. Fold the pointy nose back on itself to form the snub nose. You might try folding the nose underneath, but both ways work well.
5. Fold the whole plane lengthways, as shown.
6. Finally, fold the wings in half to complete the Bulldog Dart.

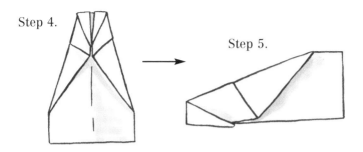

Step 4.

Step 5.

THE HARRIER

1. Fold in half lengthways to find your centre line and then fold two corners into that line, as shown.
2. Fold that top triangle down. It should look like an envelope.
3. Fold in the second set of corners. You should be able to leave a triangular point sticking out.

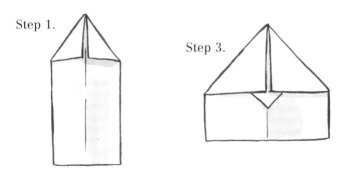

Step 1.

Step 3.

4. Fold the triangle over the corners to hold them down.
5. Fold in half along the spine, leaving the triangle on the outside, as shown.
6. Finally, fold the wings back on themselves, finding your halfway line carefully. The more care you take to be accurate with these folds, the better the plane will fly.

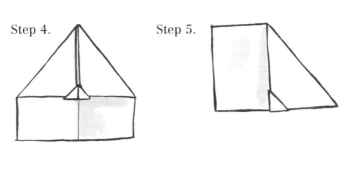

Step 4.

Step 5.

Step 6.

This plane does well at slower launch speeds. It can stall at high speed, but if you lift one of the flaps slightly at the back, it will swoop and return to your hand or fly in a great spiral. Fiddle with your plane until you are happy with it. Each one will be slightly different and have a character of its own.

THE GOLDEN AGE OF PIRACY

THERE HAVE BEEN PIRATES for as long as ships have sailed out of sight of land and law. The period known as 'the golden age' of piracy began in the seventeenth century and continued into the early eighteenth. The discovery of the new world and vast wealth there for the taking caused an explosion of privateers – some, like Francis Drake, with the complete authority and knowledge of Queen Elizabeth I.

The word 'buccaneer' comes from European sailors who caught wild pigs on the islands of Haiti and Tortuga in the Caribbean and smoked the meat on racks to preserve it. The French '*boucaner*' means to dry meat in this fashion. The men referred to themselves as the 'Brethren of the Coast' and it is from their number that the most

Thomas Tew

Stede Bonnet

Richard Worle

Jack Rackham

Blackbeard

Henry Every

Edward England

Bart Roberts (2nd)

Bart Robert.

Emanuel Wynne

Walter Kennedy

Christopher Moody

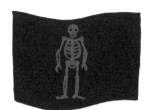

Edward Low

Christopher Condent

famous names came, like Calico Jack Rackham and Blackbeard. Perhaps the most astonishing thing about the golden age is the fact that many pirates were given pardons, sometimes in exchange for military aid or a cut of the loot. The Welsh privateer Henry Morgan was not only pardoned, but knighted by Charles II, made acting Governor of Jamaica, a vice-admiral, Commandant of the Port Royal Regiment, a Judge of the Admiralty Court and a Justice of the Peace!

Although the skull and crossbones, or 'Jolly Roger', is by far the most famous pirate flag, there were different versions and many other flags that would send fear into the hearts of merchant sailors and their captains. Above is a selection of the most famous, as well as the men who sailed under them.

GRINDING AN ITALIC NIB

—⁎—

ALTHOUGH THE PEN we used is an expensive model, this should absolutely not be tried with a valued pen. There is a reasonable chance of destroying the nib completely and the nib is usually the most expensive part to replace. The rest, after all, is just a tube.

The first thing to know is that *almost all* italic nibs are hand-ground. In theory, there is no reason why you should not be able to grind a nib to suit you, with a little common sense and care.

Before you begin, it is a good idea to get hold of an italic nib and try writing with it. The writing style is quite different and they tend to be 'scratchier'. It is extremely satisfying knowing you have ground your own nib – and the handwriting is attractive.

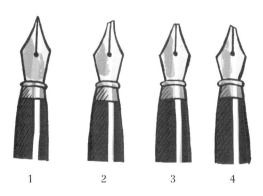

1   2   3   4

Picture 1 shows a standard nib. Picture 2 would be best suited to a left-handed writer. Picture 3 is suitable for both and 4 is best suited for right-handers. It's difficult to change from one to the other if you are not happy with the result – which is why you should try a shop-bought italic nib first.

We used a sharpening gig – a useful little gadget that helps to hold chisels at the required angle. It can be done completely by hand, but no matter how you choose to do it, stop often, dip the nib in ink and try it out. Do not be discouraged by scratching at this stage. A

fine sharpening stone will take longer, but as delicate as this is, it is probably a good idea.

GRINDING AN ITALIC NIB

You should arrive somewhere near the nib on the left – if you are left-handed. It was identical to the nib on the right before grinding. Attempts at writing with the new angle were initially discouraging. Very fine sandpaper (or wet and dry paper) was needed to smooth away roughness and dust from the grindstone. It is a matter of personal preference how far you smooth the corners, but I found it helped the easy flow of ink.

All the King's horses and all the King's men

All the King's horses and all the King's men

NOTE: This is not italic or copperplate lettering. Those alphabets have to be learned, though they are based on the wide and narrow strokes of an italic nib

FAMOUS BATTLES – PART TWO

1. Waterloo – 18 June 1815

NAPOLEON HAD OVERREACHED himself by 1814. He had lost more than 350,000 men in his march on Russia, one of the most ill-advised military actions in history. Wellington had beaten his armies and their Spanish allies in Spain. In addition, the armies of Austria and Prussia

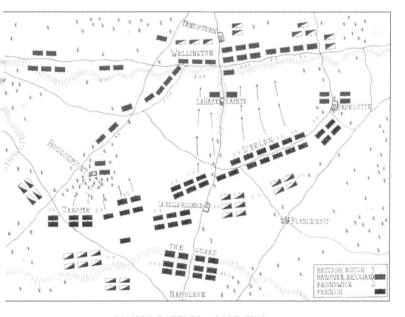

stood ready to humble him at last. Yet Napoleon was not a man to go quietly into obscurity. When he abdicated as Emperor, he was exiled to rule the tiny island of Elba off the west coast of Italy. Perhaps cruelly, he was allowed to keep the title he claimed for himself. Many lives would have been saved if he and his honour guard had stayed there. Instead, eleven months after his arrival, a frigate picked him up and he returned to France.

The French king, Louis XVIII, sent troops with orders to fire on him. Famously, Napoleon walked fearlessly out to them, threw open his coat and said, 'Let him that has the heart, kill his Emperor!' The soldiers cheered him and Napoleon turned them round and marched on Paris. By 20 March, 1815, the French king had fled and Napoleon was back. The period of March to June is still known as the 'Hundred Days' war.

With extraordinary efficiency, Napoleon put together an army of 188,000 regulars, 300,000 levies (conscripts) and another 100,000 support personnel. In addition, he had his veteran Army of the North around Paris – 124,000 men.

Wellington's Anglo-Dutch army of 95,000 was in Flanders (Belgium) at this point, with the Prussian army of 124,000 under Marshall Blücher. The Austrians had 210,000 men along the Rhine and another army of 75,000 in Italy. The Russian army of 167,000 under Barclay were coming through Germany to attack France. In many ways, Napoleon had overreached himself in 1815, as well.

Napoleon moved quickly against the armies in Belgium, attempting to crush his enemies one or two at a time.

Unfortunately for his hopes, Wellington's forces stopped one of his marshals at Quatre-Bras, south of Brussels, counter-attacking and preventing the support Napoleon needed to destroy the Prussians. Blücher's men did take terrible casualties when they met Napoleon at Ligny, but were still able to retreat in good order. Napoleon did not follow up his advantage and Wellington was able to move from Quatre-Bras to a better position, ready for battle. He chose a ridge named Mont St-Jean, to the south of the village of Waterloo. It was the evening of the 17 June and that night it rained in torrents.

Blücher had given his word to Wellington that he would reinforce the British position. His deputy Gneisenau was convinced Wellington would fail to hold the ridge and would be gone by the time the Prussians arrived. He wanted to abandon their allies and return to Prussia. Despite exhaustion and being wounded himself, the seventy-two-year-old Blücher overrode him and gave orders for his men to support Wellington. It is an interesting detail that Gneisenau arranged the Prussian marching order so that the units furthest away from Wellington would go first. It seems he knew this would delay their arrival. The furthest unit, however, was General von Bülow's IV Corps, one of the best units the Prussians had. The eventual arrival of the Prussians would force Napoleon to respond, just as he should have been attacking the British centre. This was a vital part of the victory.

The ground was a quagmire after the downpour of the night before, and Napoleon delayed the attack until it began to dry. On noon of the 18 June, he attacked at last with 72,000 against Wellington's 67,000. Napoleon's troops moved forward in a feint attack, while his 'belles filles' (beautiful daughters) guns hammered at Wellington's army for an hour. At 1 p.m., 20,000 veterans moved in line formation towards the British-held ridge. They too had to march through artillery fire and the carnage was horrific. Yet two of the veteran divisions made it to the crest through fierce hand-to-hand fighting. This was a crucial point in the battle, but it was saved by the Household Brigade and Union Brigade cavalry under the Earl of Uxbridge, who smashed the French attackers with a charge over the ridge.

The two brigades continued on across the valley, attacking the French guns. They took about twenty and most of them were exhausted as they were broken in turn by the French cavalry reserves. The damage was done, however. The only truly formidable French infantry left on the field were his Imperial Guard, his elite.

There were some confused orders in the French lines at this point. Wellington ordered his men to pull back 100 ft out of range of the French guns. Marshal Ney thought they were retreating and ordered a brigade of French cavalry to attack. His order was queried and in an angry response, Ney led them himself, taking around 4,000 cavalrymen forward without support. If Napoleon had sent in his Imperial Guard at this point, Wellington could well have lost the battle. Napoleon had become aware of the approach of the Prussians and refused to commit them.

Unsupported, the cavalry failed to damage the British square formations in any significant way. Volley fire repulsed them and the survivors eventually retreated. The heavy French cannons opened up again and more on the ridge began to die.

By four in the afternoon, the Prussians were there in force, led by the IV Corps. They took a strategic position on Napoleon's right flank and had to be dislodged by vital troops from the Imperial Young and Old Guard regiments. By the time that was done it was getting on for seven in the evening. So close to midsummer, the days were long and it was still light when Napoleon sent in his Imperial Guard at last to break the British centre. They wore dark blue jackets and wore high bearskin hats. In all their history, they had never retreated.

The Imperial Guard marched up the hill towards a brigade of British Foot Guards under Colonel Maitland and a Dutch brigade under Colonel Detmer. Volley fire and a bayonet charge made the Imperial Guard retreat. Wellington sent in more men after them as they tried to re-form and they were finished. The British Guard regiments were well aware of the reputation of the Napoleonic elite and took their hats as souvenirs. The high bearskin headgear is still worn today by the Grenadier, Welsh, Irish, Scots and Coldstream Guard regiments.

Blücher attacked the French right as Wellington counter-attacked in force. The French army collapsed. Afterwards, Blücher wanted to call the battle 'La Belle Alliance', but Wellington insisted on his old habit of naming battles after the place where he'd spent the night before. As a result, it became known as the Battle of Waterloo.

Napoleon returned to Paris and abdicated for the second time on 22 June, before surrendering to the British. HMS *Bellerophon* took him on board, one of the ships that had fought at the Nile and Trafalgar with Nelson. Ironically, *Bellerophon* (known as 'Billy Ruffian') was one of those that had fired on Napoleon's flagship *L'Orient* before she exploded at the Battle of the Nile.

Napoleon was taken to the island of St Helena and would not leave it until his death. Waterloo was Wellington's last battle, though he did become Prime Minister in 1828.

Blücher died in his bed at home in 1819.

France was forced to pay damages to Britain, Austria, Prussia and Russia. Those countries met in Vienna to settle the future of Europe. A neutral country, or buffer zone, was created from those talks, its peace guaranteed by the others. It was later known as Belgium when it became completely independent in 1830. Interestingly, it is true that the 'Wellington boot' takes its name from a leather boot style popularised by Wellington. Originally, it was made of leather and only later produced in the rubber form we know so well today.

2. Balaclava – 25 October 1854

In 1853, Tsar Nicholas I saw a chance to topple an ageing Ottoman Empire, control Turkey and extend Russian influence right into the Mediterranean. Both France and England were intent on resisting Russian encroachment on that part of the world. In a highly unusual alliance, both countries sent fleets to support Turkey.

The allied force was jointly commanded by Lord Raglan and the French Marshal Saint Arnaud. With their arrival, Turkey declared war on Russia and had some initial success before the Russians sank the Turkish fleet and invaded Bulgaria. Various skirmishes followed. Dysentery and cholera were already causing problems for the allied expeditionary force at Varna when orders arrived to take the Russian seaport of Sevastopol. The fleet of 150 warships and transports landed 51,000 French, British and Turkish soldiers thirty miles north of the port. As the cold months arrived, some of them wore woollen headgear that left only a part of the face exposed. These quickly became known as 'Balaclavas'.

On 20 September, Prince Alexander Menshikov fought them at the River Alma. His army was defeated but left almost intact as it withdrew. The allied force moved on to Sevastopol and laid siege to it while the fleet under Sir Edmund Lyons blockaded the port at sea. Menshikov decided to divert their attention from Sevastopol by attacking the main British supply base at Balaclava. He had 65,000 men and expected another 25,000 in reinforcements. In comparison, the allied forces had been reinforced to 75,000.

Balaclava is a great plain in the Crimean Peninsula with high ground in the form of the Sapoune Ridge at one end and a central spine known as the Causeway Heights. To reach the British camp at Balaclava, Menshikov had to cross the River Tchernaya and the Fedioukine Hills, coming into the North Valley. His task then was to take the British redoubts on Causeway Heights, manned by Turkish militia. Beyond them lay the British 93rd Highlanders, a thousand Royal Marines and another thousand Turkish troops, all under General Sir Colin Campbell.

The British cavalry were camped at the northern foot of the Causeway Heights to protect the flank. They were under the command of Lords Lucan and Cardigan, two men who disliked each other intensely and rarely spoke.

The battle of 25 October began when Menshikov used artillery and bayonet charges to storm three of the redoubts in two hours, routing the Turkish militia within.

The Russian cavalry burst through the allied defences and charged through the battlefield towards the suddenly defenceless British camp further south.

The only thing in their path was the 93rd Highland Regiment with Campbell. They formed a double rank as the cavalry thundered towards them and Campbell said, 'There is no retreat from here, men. You must die where you stand.' John Scott on the right, replied, 'Ay, Sir Colin. An needs be, we'll do that,' and the rest of them echoed the reponse.

They began volley fire at the oncoming wall of charging Russian horse and stood their ground until the charge collapsed against their rifle fire. It is said that one of the Highlanders was able to reach out and touch the face of a fallen mount as it lay within arm's length of him. Ever after, the stand was known as 'The Thin Red Line'.

The second main action of the day occurred when the main body of Russian horse entered the southern valley.

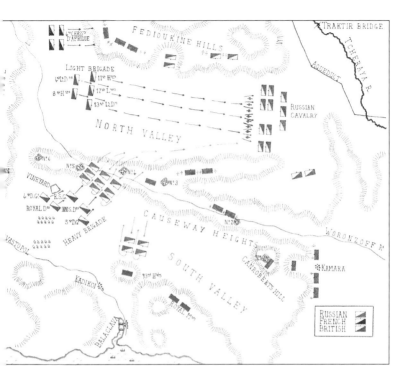

General Sir James Scarlett had brought up the Heavy Brigade at this time. The name is no exaggeration, as both men and horses were large and stronger than usual, a hammer rather than a rapier on the battlefield. General Scarlett ordered 300 of these from the 2nd and 6th Dragoons *uphill* against the Russian force of 2,000. It seemed foolhardy but the Heavy Brigade cavalry smashed through their lighter Russian counterparts, driving them from the field with almost 300 dead. The Heavy Brigade lost only ten that day, not all of them at that charge with Scarlett.

The third and final action of the day is by far the most famous. By this time, Menshikov was entrenched in the North Valley and had cannons lining the position. It was never the intention of Lord Raglan to send the Light Brigade down into the 'Valley of Death'. He saw that the guns in the captured redoubts on Causeway Heights were being removed by the Russians and sent a message to Lord Lucan that could have been better phrased. He also made the mistake of sending it with a galloper named Captain Lewis Edward Nolan, who added his own twist to the disaster.

The message to Lucan read as follows: 'Lord Raglan wishes the cavalry to advance rapidly to the front – follow the enemy and try to prevent the enemy carrying away the guns. Troop Horse Artillery may accompany. French cavalry is on your left. Immediate.'

Raglan also gave the verbal instruction: 'Tell Lord Lucan the cavalry is to attack immediately.'

Captain Nolan reached Lord Lucan with the message and passed it on. Lucan could not see the guns to which the note referred and queried which ones were meant. In exasperation, Captain Nolan replied, 'There, my lord, is your enemy, there are your guns!' and he gestured angrily in the direction of the redoubts, which was also the direction of the main Russian position. The arrogant Lucan was infuriated by the man's tone – and perhaps the implication that he was deliberately delaying going into action.

Lord Lucan ordered the Light Brigade and Lord Cardigan into the North Valley – against the wrong guns. Cardigan pointed out that three sides of the valley were covered in entrenched cannon positions, but Lucan told him haughtily that Raglan had ordered it and 'We have no choice but to obey.'

The Light Brigade were also thirsty for glory. The Heavy Brigade had seen action, but the Lights had hardly been used. Without the slightest hesitation, all 660 of them advanced into the North Valley, led by Cardigan. As the Russian guns opened up, Captain Nolan galloped alongside Cardigan, but was killed before he could point out the error.

On the north and south sides of the valley were almost fifty cannon and nineteen infantry battalions. At the end were eight more cannon pointing directly at the Light Brigade and four full Russian regiments – the entire remaining army under Menshikov.

The Light Brigade cantered at first under heavy fire, slowly building to a full gallop towards the Russian guns. Men were torn from their saddles by rifle bullets and shell fragments. The Russians could not believe what they were seeing and reacted too slowly to protect the guns once it became clear the Lights were going to make it to the end of the valley. The Cossacks around the guns panicked and ran. The Light Brigade killed any remaining gunners and then charged the Russian cavalry, driving them back. They had taken the guns, but without support could not dream of holding them. The horses were exhausted and many of the surviving men were wounded. They turned then and began to make their way back to their starting place – and the cannon fire began once more as they rode.

It took only twenty minutes, start to finish. 195 survived out of 661. Six of the then new Victoria Crosses were awarded for bravery.

The charge should be put in context. The Crimean War had its fair share of horrors, from the silent terror of cholera, to the stench of men dying of dysentery and infected wounds. It was here that Florence Nightingale introduced the idea of nursing and the concept of sanitation to a British battlefield. There were few things to lift the spirits of the British public as they read the reports. The Battle of Balaclava provided one of the most extraordinary examples of courage in warfare – equal to the Spartans at Thermopylae. You must remember that the Russians had broken before the Thin Red Line – and again against a small number of heavy cavalry. The Light Brigade faced almost fifty cannon and literally thousands of rifles and yet did not falter. As one French officer said, '*C'est magnifique, mais ce n'est pas la guerre.*' – 'It is magnificent but it is not war.' Tennyson's poem 'The Charge of the Light Brigade' is still one of the most famous pieces in the English language.

3. Rorke's Drift – 22 and 23 January 1879

The Boer Wars between Dutch and British forces were over control of lands in southern Africa, rich with diamonds, gold and timber. The Zulu armies of Shaka, then Cetewayo fought against the encroachment of their lands by both sides. Britain attempted to arrange a 'protectorate' with Cetewayo, but when he refused, they invaded Zulu lands, led by Lord Chelmsford. He entered Cetewayo's territory with only 5,000 British troops and 8,000 natives. His objective was to occupy Cetewayo's royal kraal (cattle enclosure or village), advancing on it from three directions. Accordingly, he split his force into three columns.

Chelmsford entered Zulu lands at Rorke's Drift, a farm named after its deceased owner, James Rorke. They made the farm buildings into a supply depot and moved on.

The battle of Isandlwana involved Chelmsford's No. 3 central column, a mixed force of cavalry, infantry and Royal Engineers. They had made steady progress into Zulu land, attacking a minor cattle kraal and crossing a river. Mounted troops scouted ahead to Isipezi Hill and found no sign of a Zulu force in the area, so Chelmsford decided to make a camp at Isandlwana. Perhaps because of the stony ground, he did not give orders to fortify the camp in any way.

On the morning of 22 January, Chelmsford went with about half his full force (2,500) in scouting parties, searching for signs of Zulu forces. There were many sightings as the area began to fill with Cetewayo's warriors. A message came through from the camp at Isandlwana: 'For God's sake come with all your men; the camp is surrounded and will be taken unless helped.'

By the time Chelmsford made it back to Isandlwana, the camp had been overrun and 1,300 men killed. The defenders had fought bravely, but a Zulu force of 10,000 had

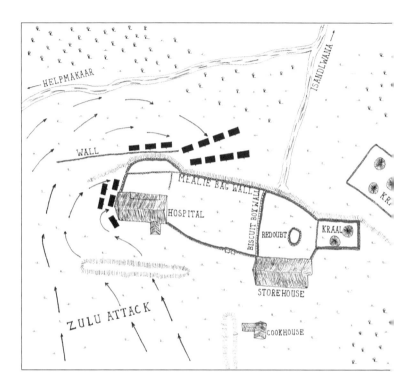

attacked with ferocious energy, using their assegai spears to cut their way in, despite rifle fire and bayonets. They lost about 3,000 warriors in the attack.

Chelmsford did not believe this could have happened at first. Not everyone under his command had been killed – about 55 British and 300 natives survived, while the Zulus paraded in the red uniforms and raided the stores before moving off. The whole area was filled with hostile impis (attack groups), right back to Rorke's Drift. Chelmsford chose to retreat back to the border. His small column formed a hostile camp for the night and as darkness fell, they saw the flames of Rorke's Drift in the distance. It too had been attacked by the warriors of Cetewayo that day.

The main house at Rorke's Drift had been converted into a hospital as well as a supply store. It had eleven rooms, stone exterior walls and a thatched roof. There was also a stone walled chapel being used as a store, and a few other outbuildings in the compound. When firing was heard on the morning of 22 January, an evacuation was considered, but the extra-ordinary speed of the Zulu impis across open ground meant that any attempt to move the sick and injured would be overtaken. Although they only had a hundred men fit to fight, the decision was taken to fortify the compound and wait it out.

A Zulu impi of 4,500, under Prince Dabulamanzi kaM-pande, attacked the compound late in the afternoon. Their assegais could not reach through the piled grain bags and biscuit boxes at first and they were thrown back by point-blank rifle fire. The initial attacks were unsuccessful before they managed to set fire to the hospital building, get in and start killing the helpless patients. Private Alfred Henry Hook used his bayonet to hold them back while Private John Williams cut through an internal wall and pulled the sick and injured through to relative safety.

The battle raged on all day and long into the night

before the Zulus finally moved on at dawn on the 23 January. They left four to five hundred of their dead around the barricaded compound. The British had lost 17 dead and 10 seriously wounded. For the individual acts of bravery during the siege, eleven Victoria Crosses were awarded to the following: Lieutenants Chard and Bromhead, Privates Alfred Hook, Frederick Hitch, Robert Jones, William Jones, James Dalton, John Williams and Corporal Allen. Surgeon James Reynolds was awarded his VC for tending to the wounded under fire. Christian Schiess received the first VC awarded to a soldier serving in the Natal Native force. He was a Swiss volunteer and had killed three men in hand-to-hand fighting, preventing a break into the main house.

You could do a lot worse than seeing the film *Zulu*, with Michael Caine playing Lieutenant Bromhead. It gives an idea of the sort of extraordinary bravery witnessed on both sides of this conflict.

4. *The Somme*

One of the many and complex reasons that World War I began was that Germany invaded Belgium. Britain was bound by treaty to defend the country. Similar alliances across Europe drew in all the great powers one by one. It may have begun with the assassination of Archduke Franz Ferdinand in Serbia, but that was merely the spark that set the world on fire.

The Somme was the river in France that Edward III crossed just before the battle of Crécy. The area has had a great deal of British blood soaking into its earth over the centuries, but never more so than on the first day of the Battle of the Somme, 1 July 1916.

Before the British army marched into the machine-gun tracks criss-crossing the battlefield, General Sir Douglas Haig had ordered eight days of artillery bombardment.

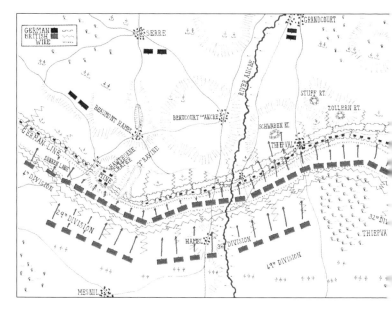

This had not proved a successful tactic over the previous two years and it did not on that day. One flaw was that the barrage had to stop to allow the allies to advance, so as soon as it stopped, the Germans knew the attack was coming and made their preparations. They had solid, deep bunkers of concrete and wood that resisted the barrage very well indeed. Their barbed-wire emplacements were also still intact after the shells stopped.

At 7.28 in the morning, the British forces detonated two huge mines, then three smaller ones near German lines. The idea was probably to intimidate the enemy, but instead, they acted as a final confirmation of the attack.

The slaughter began at 7.30, when the British soldiers rose up out of their trenches and tried to cross 800 yards in the face of machine-gun fire. A few actually made it to the German front line in that first surge before they were cut down. There were 60,000 British casualties and 19,000 dead. An entire generation fell on a single morning, making it the worst disaster of British military history. Who can say what their lives would have meant and achieved had they survived?

There is a touching poem called 'For the Fallen' written by Laurence Binyon in 1914 that is quoted at every Remembrance Day service. This is an extract from it, remembering those who gave their lives for their country. The second verse is particularly poignant.

They went with songs to the battle, they were young,
Straight of limb, true of eye, steady and aglow.
They were staunch to the end against odds uncounted:
They fell with their faces to the foe.

They shall grow not old, as we that are left grow old:
Age shall not weary them, nor the years condemn.
At the going down of the sun and in the morning
We will remember them.

UNDERSTANDING GRAMMAR – PART THREE: VERBS AND TENSES

⌁ Transitive and Intransitive Verbs ⌁

How often will you need to know the difference? Hardly ever, or not at all, but the odd thing is that those who do know these fiddly bits of grammar take *enormous* satisfaction from that knowledge.

Transitive verbs are verbs that must have an object. For example, 'to bury', 'to distract', 'to deny' and many more. You simply cannot write them without an object – 'John denied', 'Susan buried'. John has to deny *something* and Susan has to bury something for it to make sense.

Intransitive verbs are verbs that can be complete without an object: 'to arrive', 'to digress', 'to exist'.

Some verbs can be transitive or intransitive, depending on how they are used in a sentence (just to make things harder): 'The fire burns' (intransitive). 'The fire has burned my finger' (transitive – 'my finger' is the object). 'He has broken the glass' (transitive). 'Glass breaks easily' (intransitive).

Again, though, this is not calculating parabolic orbits –

recognising whether a verb is used transitively or intransitively is a matter of care, common sense and memory.

⌁ The Tenses ⌁

It will come as no surprise to hear that verbs need forms expressing the past, present and future. There are important differences between someone saying 'They have closed the gate' and 'They will close the gate.' The three *principal* forms of verbs, therefore, express these differences. They are known as Present Tense, Past Tense and Future Tense.

The Present Tense

There are five forms for a verb in the Present Tense:

1. Present Simple – *I write.*
2. Present Emphatic – *I do write.*
3. Present Continuous – *I am writing.*
4. Present Perfect Continuous – *I have been writing.*
5. Present Perfect – *I have written.*

The Present Emphatic form, 'I do write', may look a bit odd. It is mostly used in negative statements ('You don't care, do you?') and in questions ('Do you care?') and strong, emphatic statements ('I do care!').

Sometimes, the present can be used to talk about the future – 'I go to London next week' or 'When he arrives, he will hear the news' – but the meaning is clear from context, as it is here: 'Tomorrow, I'm going to the shops.'

The Present Perfect 'I have written' form may also look out of place at first glance. It is used in sentences like the following: '*When I have written this*, I will come and speak to you.' This is clearly an action that is going on in the present, coming from the past.

Similarly, Present Perfect Continuous: '*I have been writing* all my life,' – again, an action which is going on in the general present, if not at that exact moment.

The Past Tense

The Past Tense is usually formed by adding 'd' or 'ed' to the verb (love, *loved*; alter, *altered)*; changing the vowel sound (swim, *swam*; throw, *threw)*; or remaining the same as the present tense (put, *put*; cast, *cast*).

When the verb ends in a single consonant after a short vowel with the stress on the last syllable, the final consonant is doubled before the 'ed' ending (refer, *referred*; fan, *fanned*).

If the letter 'y' ends the word after a consonant, it becomes 'i' before the 'ed' ending (try, *tried*; cry, *cried*).

You'll probably be able to find exceptions to these rules. English has taken so many words from other languages that no rules apply to all of them. However, these work well on most occasions.

There are four standard forms for the past tense:

1. Simple Past – *I wrote.*
2. Past Continuous – *I was writing.*
3. Past Perfect (Pluperfect) – *I had written.*
4. Past Perfect Continuous – *I had been writing.*

There are also a couple of specific constructions, like 'used to', that work in sentences about the past. '*I used to* write about relationships, but now...' Clearly, the writing took place in the past.

Similarly, adding 'going to' is a common construction: 'I was going to call you, but I forgot.' The intention of calling took place in the past.

The Future Tense

First a note on 'shall', a peculiar little word. It is often used interchangeably with 'will'. It survives in commandments as 'Thou shalt not kill.' Its main use is in expressing a future wish. The fairy godmother says 'You *shall* go to the ball!' to Cinderella.

One distinction between 'will' and 'shall' is that 'shall' implies some choice. When I was a boy, I was taught that only God could say 'I will go to the shops' as only he could be certain. The rest of us should say 'I shall go to the shops' because we could be hit by a bus, and not actually make it there. Admittedly, that example rather misses the point that being killed is a little more important than errors of grammar, but it was memorable at least.

The four forms for future time are:

1. Simple Future – *I will write.*
2. Future Continuous – *I will be writing.*
3. Future Perfect – *I will have written*
4. Future Perfect Continuous: *I will have been writing.*

There is also a construction using 'am going to', as in 'I am going to kill you', and various other minor constructions using adverbs of time: 'I am going home *tomorrow*', or adverbial phrases such as 'The bus leaves *in ten minutes*.'

...and that is about it for tenses.

If you've come this far, we know you'll be disappointed if we stop it there. 'What about modal verbs? What about the subjunctive?' you will say to yourself. Prepare to be thrilled at the final two sections. This is the gold standard. Take it slowly.

◡◠ Modal Auxiliary Verbs ◡◠

Modal auxiliary verbs are irregular auxiliary verbs – the sort of verbs that give English a reputation for complexity. The language has many auxiliary combinations, mostly using 'to be' and 'to have' in combination with another verb: 'I *am* going', 'I *have been* watching' and so on.

Modal auxiliary verbs are often used to express the speaker's attitude 'You shouldn't do that', or as a conditional tense: 'Don't go any closer. *He could be dangerous*.'

You use them all the time, however, so do not be too worried. Here is a list of them:

will, *would*, *shall*, *should*, *may*, *might*, *can*, *could*, *must*, *dare*, *need*, *ought*
won't, *wouldn't*, *shan't*, *shouldn't*, *mayn't*, *mightn't*, *can't*, *couldn't*, *mustn't*, *daren't*, *needn't*, *oughtn't*

Note that the use of 'need' as a modal verb, as in 'Need we do this?', is not that common, whereas 'needn't' is used quite regularly: 'He needn't enjoy it, as long as he eats it!'

Modal verbs have no infinitive or '-ing' form – 'to should' or 'maying' do not exist. There is no 's' form of the third person – 'he can' not 'he cans'. They do not stand on their own and are always used in conjunction with other verbs – 'May I go to the cinema?'

⟅ The Subjunctive ⟆

The **Indicative** mood is the standard factual style of modern English: 'I walked into the park.' The **Subjunctive** mood tends to appear in more formal English, when we wish to express the importance of something. This leads on from the modal verbs, as it too often expresses a wish, an uncertainty or a possibility. It is frequently formed using modal auxiliaries: 'If only they would come!' This is a complex form and scholarly works have been written on the subjunctive alone. With the limitations of space, we can merely dip a toe.

Present Subjunctive

In the present subjunctive, all verbs look like the infinitive but without the 'to' – 'do' not 'to do' – and they don't take an extra 's', even in the third person: 'We demand that *he do* the job properly.'

The verb 'to be' provides the most commonly used

examples of the subjunctive form. In the present subjunctive, following the rule in the previous paragraph, 'be' is used: 'Even if that *be* the official view, I must act.' In the simple past subjunctive, we use 'were' throughout. Example: 'If he *were* sorry, he'd have apologised by now.'

Here are some examples of classic subjunctive expressions: 'Be that as it may', 'If I were a rich man,' 'Suffice it to say', 'Come what may', 'God save the Queen', 'If I were the only girl in the world.'

The subjunctive is also used in sentences beginning 'If...', as long as the subject is expressing a wish, an uncertainty or a possibility: 'If I were twenty years younger, I would ask you to dance.'

Lady Nancy Astor once said to Winston Churchill, 'Winston, if I were your wife, I'd put poison in your coffee.' He replied, 'Nancy, If I were your husband, I'd drink it.'

The subjunctive should *not* be used when the 'If...' construction is a simple conditional: '*If you are ill*, the doctor will make you better'. 'If' is used here to indicate that one event is conditional on another. There is no sense of a wish or possibility. 'If my doctor treats you, he will cure you' is another example of a simple indicative conditional. The speaker is expressing a fact conditional on the arrival of the doctor, rather than a speculative possibility.

The subjunctive is also used in certain types of sentence containing 'that':

1. They demanded *that he take* every precaution.
2. It is essential *that they be* brought back for punishment.

3. I must recommend *that this law be* struck from the books.

Past Subjunctive

In the past subjunctive, all verbs take the common form of the simple past tense. 'Have' becomes 'had', 'know' becomes 'knew' and so on. As mentioned above, 'to be' is a little different as it becomes 'were' (and not 'was'), but all the others are regular. Here are some examples:

1. He wept as if *he were being squeezed*.
2. I wish *you were* here!
3. If only *I had worked* in school.

Note that these can be indistinguishable from the standard past perfect 'had worked', as in the table below. The 'If only...' and 'I wish...' beginnings suggest subjunctive.

The following table is almost the end of the grammar section. It covers the subjunctive in all the major tenses, using examples from the verb 'to work' throughout. The important thing to remember is that it might look complicated, but *there is only one form of subjunctive for each verb tense*. If the example is 'I work', then all six persons of the verb use that form.

Mind you, don't expect to 'get it' immediately – this is one of the really tricky forms of English. The answer, however, is not to stop teaching it and watch it wither away as generations come through school with little knowledge of their own language. The answer to difficulty is always to get your hands around its throat and hold on until you have reached an understanding. Luckily, this is happening – especially in America. The subjunctive is on its way back.

Tense	Indicative	Subjunctive
Simple present	*He works*	*He work*
Present continuous	*She is working*	*She be working*
Present perfect	*He has worked*	*He have worked*
Present perfect continuous	*It has been working*	*It have been working*
Simple past	*We worked*	*We worked*
Past continuous	*I was working*	*I were working*
Past perfect	*They had worked*	*They had worked*
Past perfect continuous	*We had been working*	*We had been working*

In addition, here are eight simple sentences in the sub-junctive. It is perhaps more common than you realise. Read each one and see how the subjunctive form of the verb is used.

1. He acts as if *he knew* you.
2. I would rather *you had given* a different answer.
3. If only *we had* a home to go to!
4. I wish *I could run* as fast as my older brother.
5. Would that *you were* my friend.
6. I suggest that *he leave.*
7. Thy Kingdom *come,* thy will *be* done.
8. If one green bottle *should* accidentally *fall…*

Now go back to the beginning of Grammar Part One and read it all again.

BUILDING A WORKBENCH

✦

BEFORE WE COULD MAKE a number of the things in this book, it was obvious we needed a workbench. Even the simplest task in a workshop becomes difficult without a solid vice and a flat surface.

We kept this as simple as possible. Pine is easiest to cut, but it also breaks, dents and crushes, which is why classic workbenches are made out of beech – a very hard wood.

Complete beginners should start with pine, as mistakes are a *lot* cheaper. Planning is crucial – every table is different. Ours fitted the wall of the workshop and is higher than almost any workbench you'll ever see. Both of us are tall and prefer to work at a higher level. Draw the plan and have an idea of how much wood you will need.

The suppliers cut the wood square to save time and we spent two days cutting mortice and tenon joints before assembling it.

RULE: Measure twice and cut once. Carpentry is 80% care and common sense, 20% skill, or even artistry. You do not have to be highly skilled to make furniture, as long as you *never* lose your temper, plan carefully and practise, practise, practise. The reason a professional is better than an amateur is because the professional cuts joints every day.

MORTICE AND TENON JOINTS

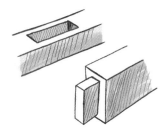

A mortice is a trench cut into wood. The tenon is the piece that fits into the trench.

NOTE: Using sharp tools is not to be undertaken lightly. A chisel will remove a finger as easily as a piece of wood. Don't try this unless you have an adult willing to show you the basics. There are hundreds of fiddly little things (like how to hold a chisel) that we couldn't fit in here.

We started by making two rectangular frames to go at each end of the table workbench. This is a very simple design, but mortice and tenon joints are strong on the corners.

Make sure that the top of your tenon is not too close to

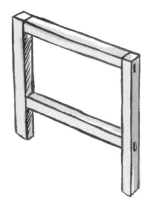

the top of the upright. When it comes to cutting the mortice, you do not want to break through.

For simple 'through' joints, the tenon length is the same as the width of the upright. To create the tenon, you have to make four saw cuts (accurately!) down to a marked line that is equal to the depth of the upright. In the picture, only the middle rectangle will remain. After the four cuts, you saw away the waste pieces and use a chisel to trim any splinters or roughness.

When you have your tenons cut, number them in pencil. Use the tenons as the template for the mortice trenches, also numbered. We also pencilled a cross on the top side so we wouldn't lose track. Obviously, they should all be identical, but it's odd how often they aren't. Mark the mortices with extreme care, taking note of the exact position. The first upright will be relatively easy, but the second has to be absolutely identical – and that's where the problems creep in.

Next, cut the mortice. Great care is needed here – and some skill with the chisel. Take care also not to crush the edges as you lever backwards. Ideally, you should use a chisel as wide as the mortice itself – though some prefer to use narrower blades.

Once you have your pair of end pieces, you need bars running lengthways to prevent wobble. We used mortice and tenons again, as the beech joints seemed easily strong enough for our needs.

In the picture, you can see that we put both beams on one side. We wanted to have access for storage underneath, so we left the front open.

The rope arrangement in the picture is called a 'windlass'. It is used when a piece of furniture is too long to be clamped. Most tables will have this problem and it's good to know you can overcome it with nothing more than a double length of rope and a stick to twist it tighter and tighter. The same technique has even been used to pull wooden ships out of the sea. Be sure to protect the wood with cloth, or you'll cut grooves into your uprights.

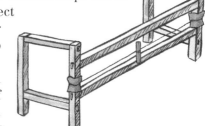

The top planks can be glued together if they have perfect edges, or simply screwed in place. The simplest possible method is to screw down into the end pieces, but this does leave ugly screw heads visible. We used a corner piece underneath, screwing across into the end piece and also up into the underside of the top. It worked well enough for our purposes.

To finish, we sanded like madmen for the best part of a day, used filler for the gaps we could not explain in the joints, then wiped it all over with linseed oil. The oil soaked in very nicely to seal the wood – just in case we spill paint on it in the future.

SAMPLING SHAKESPEARE

———✦———

No WRITER OF ANY AGE has come close to rivalling the creative genius of William Shakespeare. He was born in 1564, on 23 April – St George's Day, in Stratford-upon-Avon. Anyone alive should know *Macbeth*, *Romeo and Juliet*, *A Midsummer Night's Dream*, *King Lear*, *Othello* and *Hamlet*, or have seen them in a theatre.

Here are a few of the better-known quotations. Shakespeare has added countless commonly used phrases and words to English – so common in fact, that we often hardly recognise them as Shakespearean. He really did write 'I have not slept one wink' before anyone else, as well as 'I will wear my heart upon my sleeve' and hundreds more.

1.

What's in a name? that which we call a rose
by any other word would smell as sweet.

Romeo and Juliet, Act 2, Scene 2

2.

This royal throne of kings, this sceptered isle,
This earth of majesty, this seat of Mars,
This other Eden, demi-paradise,
This fortress built by Nature for herself
Against infection and the hand of war,

This happy breed of men, this little world,
This precious stone set in the silver sea,
Which serves it in the office of a wall,
Or as a moat defensive to a house,
Against the envy of less happier lands,
This blessed plot, this earth, this realm, this England.

Richard II, Act 2, Scene 1

3.

If music be the food of love, play on.

Twelfth Night, Act 1, Scene 1

4.

But screw your courage to the sticking-place,
And we'll not fail.

Macbeth, Act 1, Scene 7

5.

Out, out brief candle!
Life's but a walking shadow, a poor player
That struts and frets his hour upon the stage,
And then is heard no more; it is a tale
Told by an idiot, full of sound and fury,
Signifying nothing.

Macbeth, Act 5, Scene 5

6.

Cry 'Havoc!' and let slip the dogs of war.

Julius Caesar, Act 3, Scene 1

7.

Once more unto the breach, dear friends, once more;
Or close the wall up with our English dead!

Henry V, Act 3, Scene 1

8.

Neither a borrower, nor a lender be;
For loan oft loses both itself and friend.

Hamlet, Act 1, Scene 3

9.

All the world's a stage,
And all the men and women merely players.

As You Like It, Act 2, Scene 7

10.

Uneasy lies the head that wears a crown.

Henry IV, Part 2, Act 3, Scene 1

11.

The lady doth protest too much, methinks.

Hamlet, Act 3, Scene 2

12.

> To be, or not to be: that is the question:
> Whether 'tis nobler in the mind to suffer
> The slings and arrows of outrageous fortune,
> Or to take arms against a sea of troubles,
> And by opposing end them?

Hamlet, Act 3, Scene 1

13.

> Let me have men about me that are fat;
> Sleek-headed men and such as sleep o'nights.
> Yond Cassius has a lean and hungry look;
> He thinks too much: such men are dangerous.

Julius Caesar, Act 1, Scene 2

14.

> We are such stuff
> As dreams are made on, and our little life
> Is rounded with a sleep.
> [Usually rendered as '...dreams are made of']

The Tempest, Act 4, Scene 1

15.

Why, then the world's mine oyster,
Which I with sword will open.

The Merry Wives of Windsor,
Act 2, Scene 2

16.

I am a man
More sinn'd against than sinning.

King Lear, Act 3, Scene 2

17.

There's a divinity that shapes our ends,
Rough-hew them how we will.

Hamlet, Act 5, Scene 2

18.

There are more things in heaven and earth, Horatio,
Than are dreamt of in your philosophy.

Hamlet, Act 1, Scene 5

19.

Something is rotten in the state of Denmark.

Hamlet, Act 1, Scene 4

20.

Double, double toil and trouble;
Fire burn and cauldron bubble.

Macbeth, Act 4, Scene 1

21.

Is this a dagger which I see before me,
The handle toward my hand?

Macbeth, Act 2, Scene 1

22.

Yet do I fear thy nature;
It is too full o' the milk of human kindness.

Macbeth, Act 1, Scene 5

23.

Why, man, he doth bestride the narrow world
Like a Colossus.

Julius Caesar, Act 1 Scene 2

24.

Et tu, Brute!

Julius Caesar, Act 3, Scene 1

25.

This was the most unkindest cut of all.

Julius Caesar, Act 3, Scene 2

26.
  Good-night, good-night! parting is such sweet sorrow.

  Romeo and Juliet, Act 2, Scene 2

27.
  A plague o' both your houses!

  Romeo and Juliet, Act 3, Scene 1

28.
  Now is the winter of our discontent.

  Richard III, Act 1, Scene 1

29.
  We few, we happy few, we band of brothers.

  Henry V, Act 4, Scene 3

30.
  I thought upon one pair of English legs
  Did march three Frenchmen.

  Henry V, Act 3, Scene 6

EXTRAORDINARY STORIES – PART THREE

<hr style="width:20%; text-align:center; margin-left:auto; margin-right:auto;" />

Touching the Void

IN MAY 1985, two young English climbers set off to conquer the unclimbed west face of Siula Grande – a 21,000-foot (6,400 m) peak in the Andes. There are no mountain rescue services in such a remote region, but Joe Simpson (25) and Simon Yates (21) were experienced, confident and very fit. Their story is an extraordinary one. Apart from being made into a book and a film, it has inspired intense debate among that small group of expert climbers with experience enough to judge what happened.

The two men tackled the face in one fast push, roped together and taking everything they needed with them. They carried ice axes and wore boots with spikes (crampons), using ice screws and ropes for the ascent.

They climbed solidly that first day until darkness fell and they dug a snow cave and slept. All the second day, they climbed sheet ice, reaching 20,000 feet when high winds and a blizzard hit them on an exposed vertical slope. At that point, they were climbing flutes of powder snow, the most treacherous of surfaces and incredibly dangerous. It took five to six hours to climb just 200 feet in the dark before they found a safe place for a second snow cave.

The third morning began with a clear blue sky. By 2 p.m., they reached the north ridge at last – the first men ever to climb that face of Siula Grande. Both men felt exhausted after some of the hardest climbing of their lives, but they decided to follow the ridge towards the peak.

They reached it, but with the weather uncertain, they couldn't stay for long. Only half an hour into the descent, clouds came in and they were lost in a whiteout on the ridge, completely blind. On one side was a drop of thousands of feet and the ridge itself was made of overhanging cornices of snow that could break off under their weight. Yates saw the ridge through a break in the clouds and climbed back up to it. The cornice broke under his weight and he fell, saved by the rope attached to Simpson. He shouted up that he had found the ridge. In such conditions, progress was very slow. By the time darkness came, they were still at 20,000 feet.

The fourth day began with good weather once more. The two men came to a cut in the ridge and Simpson started to climb down a face of sheer ice. He hammered in one of his ice axes and didn't like the sound it made. As he pulled one out to get a better contact, the other gave way without warning and he fell.

He hit hard, his shinbone going through his knee and into the upper leg. As Yates climbed down, he tried to stand on it, appalled at the pain and grating of the bones. The two men looked at each other in desperation. Simpson expected his friend to leave him. There was no other choice – a broken leg so far from civilisation meant that he was dead. Instead, Yates stayed and they discussed a plan to lower Simpson on two ropes, knotted together. Yates would dig himself a seat in the snow and lower Simpson the first 150 feet. The knot wouldn't pass through the lowering device, so Simpson would dig in until Yates had retied it and could lower away once more.

The laborious process began, with Simpson face down. His broken leg jarred constantly, but it had to be fast as neither their endurance nor the light would last for long. Yates's snow seats crumbled quickly in the time it took to lower his friend. As the hours passed, a full storm hit the mountain with wind chill of –80 degrees. Darkness came upon them and both men were exhausted. They had no gas to make tea or get warm. They continued on in the dark, one rope at a time.

Simpson felt the powder snow change to hard ice and called out to stop. His voice wasn't heard and he slipped over the edge of an overhang, dangling below it. He couldn't reach a surface and, crucially, was unable to take his weight off the rope. Above him in the dark, Yates waited alone and freezing, with the wind roaring around him.

At first, Simpson attempted to climb back up the rope using a 'prussic loop', a knot that locks solid once pressure is applied. He needed two and managed to fix the first with frozen hands. The second one escaped his numb fingers and he watched it fall with his last hopes. He waited then to drag Yates to his death.

Yates waited and waited as his seat began to crumble under the unrelenting weight. All he could do was hang on until he began to slide down. He remembered he had a penknife and made a decision in an instant, using it to cut the rope. The rope snaked away and below the overhang, Simpson fell into darkness, losing consciousness. Yates dug himself a snow cave out of the storm and waited for daylight.

Simpson awoke in pitch blackness on a narrow slope, sliding. He had fallen more than a hundred feet into a crevasse, ending up on an ice ledge next to another drop into infinite darkness. He screwed in an ice screw anchor very quickly.

His helmet torch revealed the rope going up to a small hole eighty feet above. He thought Yates was on the end of it, dead. Simpson thought the rope would come tight on Yates' body. He pulled it to him and it fell. When he saw the end, he knew it had been cut and guessed what had happened. He was pleased Yates was alive, but realised his own chances of survival had dropped to almost nothing.

In the dark, he turned off the torch to save the batteries. Alone, he despaired.

Yates continued to climb down the next day, feeling desperately guilty about cutting the rope. He lowered himself past the overhang and the crevasse, convinced that Simpson was dead. He went on numbly, following tracks back to the base camp that he had made with Simpson only days before.

When no one answered his shouts, Simpson tried to climb out of his crevasse, but eighty feet of sheer ice was impossible with only one working leg. He didn't believe anyone would ever find him. His only course seemed to be to sit and wait to die – or to lower himself into the crevasse to see if there was another way out in the darkness below. He took this terrifying decision, but didn't put a knot on the end of the rope. He decided that if he reached the end and there was nothing beneath him, he would rather fall than be stuck and slowly freeze.

Joe lowered himself eighty feet and found he was in an hourglass-shaped crevasse. He reached the pinch point and found a crust of snow there that had a chance of taking his weight. He heard cracking and movement beneath him, but there was light nearby, at the top of a slope he thought he could climb, bad leg or not. This was the way out.

Though every jarring step brought him close to fainting, he made it onto the mountain-side to see a blue sky and bright sunshine. He lay there and laughed with relief at his deliverance.

After the initial exhilaration, he looked further down and realised that he still had miles of glacier to cross as well as a treacherous maze of crevasses. He thought at first that he couldn't do it, but there was no point in simply sitting and waiting. He could see Yates' tracks and knew that they would lead him through the crevasse field.

He made progress sitting down, with his legs flat on the snow and pushing himself along backwards. Snow and high winds came again, and he kept going as darkness fell, terrified at losing sight of Simon's tracks.

The tracks had gone by the morning of the sixth day, but Simpson struggled on, reaching at last the jumbled boulders that meant the end of the glacier. He wrapped his sleeping mat around the broken leg, using his ice axes to try and support himself over the broken ground. He fell at almost every step and each fall was like breaking the leg again. Somehow, he kept going. He ate snow for water, but there was never enough to quench a brutal thirst. He could hear streams running under the rocks, but maddeningly he could not find them. He pushed himself on and on until he collapsed and lay looking at the sky as it grew dark once more.

As Day 7 dawned, he could barely move at first. He believed he was going to die, but kept crawling. He found a trickle of water and drank litres of it, feeling it make him stronger. Despite this, he was becoming delirious.

Simpson reached the lake by the camp by four in the afternoon of the seventh day. He knew the camp was in a valley at the far end, but he had no idea if Yates would be there. He tried to make faster progress, plagued by the thought that he would get there too late.

Clouds came down as the day progressed and by the time he looked into the valley, it was white with mist. He lay there for a long time, delirious and hallucinating. Eventually, he moved on as night fell and it began to snow once more.

He dragged himself through the latrine area of the camp and the sharp smell acted like smelling salts, bringing him back. He began to call for Yates and when no one came at first, he believed he had been left behind.

Yet Simon Yates had stayed and he woke as he heard his name called. When he heard his name again, he went out and began to search. He found his friend a couple of hundred yards from the camp and dragged him back to the tent. Yates could not believe it. He had cut the rope and seen the drop and the crevasse. He *knew* Simpson could not have survived.

As Joe Simpson became conscious, he sought to ease his friend's guilt. His first words were,

'Don't worry, I would have done the same.'

Adapted from *Touching the Void* by Joe Simpson, published by Jonathan Cape

NAVAL FLAG CODES

In 1800, *Telegraphic Signals, or Marine Vocabulary* was published by Sir Home Popham, a Royal Navy captain. Before this point, there were crude systems available, so that messages such as 'Enemy in Sight' could be passed along the ships of the line. Sir Home Popham's system was extremely simple to use.

Just ten flags could be used to represent all the letters of the alphabet. The first ten were shown by one flag. Each letter after could be shown by two flags read from the top down – 1 and 3 to make the thirteenth letter, for example. An extra flag was needed for nought to make numbers like 10 and 20. For added efficiency, Popham made the number 9 flag represent both 'I' and 'J' – a letter only rarely used.

A 'substitution' flag was used for numbers like 11 and 22, as only one of each type was available.

Finally 'preparation' and 'finishing' flags were needed to signal the beginning and end of a message.

Spelling every word of a long message would have been dangerously time-consuming, especially in a complex sea battle. Popham came up with code combinations. 'Expects' was No. 269, for example. If a word was not in the codebook, such as the name of a small port, it could of course be spelled out. With telescopes, it was possible for admirals to contact their captains over vast distances – a

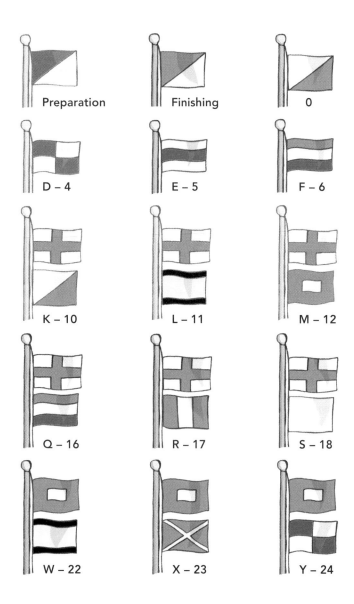

Preparation

Finishing

0

D – 4

E – 5

F – 6

K – 10

L – 11

M – 12

Q – 16

R – 17

S – 18

W – 22

X – 23

Y – 24

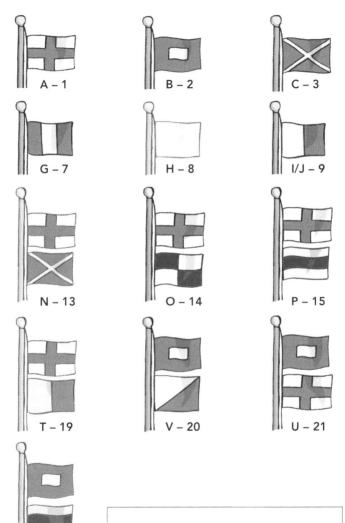

A – 1

B – 2

C – 3

G – 7

H – 8

I/J – 9

N – 13

O – 14

P – 15

T – 19

V – 20

U – 21

Z – 25

Try making your own name in flags

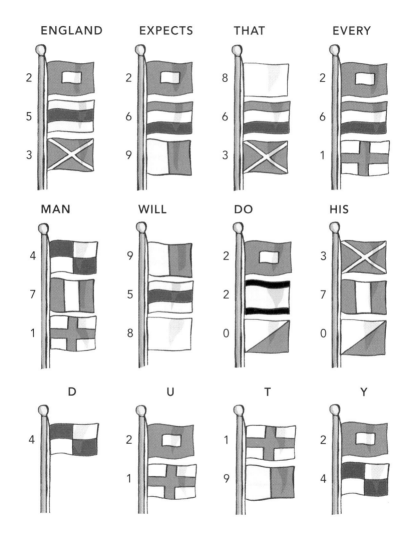

crucial part of large-scale battles at sea. At night, the system was recreated in lights, though in a simpler form.

The most famous message of all is the one sent by Admiral Horatio Nelson at the Battle of Trafalgar in 1805, just off the south-west coast of Spain. On the morning of 20 October, he invited his friend Vice Admiral Collingwood and other captains to have dinner with him on *Victory*. Amongst those invited was John Cooke of the *Bellerophon*. As the ship left her place in the line to approach Nelson's ship, *Bellerophon*'s first lieutenant saw signal '370' flying from *Mars,* the next ship in the line. Number 370 is 'Enemy Coming out of Port'. Before *Bellerophon* could relay the message, *Victory* acknowledged, having seen the signal. Nelson cancelled the dinner and called for 'General Chase – south-east.'

With the enemy ships in sight, Nelson decided to send this message to his captains: 'Nelson confides that every man will do his duty.' One of his officers suggested changing 'Nelson' to 'England' and Nelson agreed the change, crossing to Lieutenant Pasco who would send the flag combinations. He told Pasco it must be quick, as he wanted to send his old favourite 'Engage the enemy more closely'. Pasco suggested that 'confides' be changed to 'expects'. 'Expects' was in the signals book, but 'confides' would have had to be spelled out. Nelson replied, 'That will do, Pasco; make it directly.'

(Note that the 'Y' of 'duty' is 24 and not 25 because of the double use of 'I'/'J'. Also, in the eighteenth century, the alphabet put 'U' after 'V' and not before it, as we do today. That is why the 'U' of 'duty' is number 21.)

On seeing this signal, cheers could be heard throughout the fleet. When his famous 'Engage the enemy more closely' went up next, the cheers were heard again.

WRAPPING A PARCEL IN BROWN PAPER AND STRING

NOT A VERY 'DANGEROUS' ACTIVITY, it's true, but it is extremely satisfying to know how to do this. There are two main ways: one without sticky tape of any kind and a more ornate one that needs the ends held with tape. I think they both have a place when sending a present or something thoughtful to someone else – just to give them the old-fashioned pleasure of tearing it open. It is true that you could simply cocoon a parcel in tape, but there is a certain elegance in doing it without.

You will need brown paper and string, available from most post offices and all stationers.

Place the item to be posted on the sheet and cut a piece to fit it. Leave as much as half the height again and three times the width. Be generous rather than mean with the paper. If it really is too much, you can cut some off later, but you can never put it back on.

If you were using sticky tape, you'd use less paper, fold one sheet under the other and then tape the edge. Here, we are going to fold the edge down over itself in strips. This will create a 'spine' of paper that is very useful for rigidity and finishing it off. It also looks quite good, if you are careful with the folds.

Take a little time getting the ends right. Fold in a middle piece on each side, so that you end up with a duck's bill in brown paper, as in the picture. This is not the classic 'folding triangles in on themselves' technique. It is better.

Fold that duck's bill over itself into a neat point on both ends. You

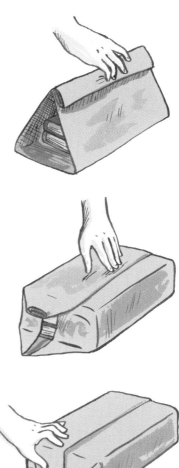

don't need to tape it, just leave it loose. The folded spine will prove very useful to hold it all together while you tie the string.

Now for the string. Cut a good long bit – three or four feet (90–120 cm). Once again, you can always shorten it. Begin on the side where the final knot or bow will go. Take the string around to the other side and then cross the two pieces as shown above, changing directions at ninety degrees. Take the two lines round the other ends of the parcel and back to the middle of where you started, for tying. It is helpful to have someone put their finger on the knot to stop it slipping.

One useful tip is to tie an extra knot before tying the final bow, linking the two lines together on top.

WRAPPING A PARCEL IN BROWN PAPER AND STRING

This makes it more secure and is a good habit to get into.

The spine of folded paper is underneath. The parcel is neatly wrapped. Well done.

The only drawback to this method is that the crossed strings go right through where you would usually put the address. It is possible to tie the string so that it doesn't, but we found this way needed a bit of tape to hold those ends down.

Instead of starting in the middle of the parcel, start at one end, running the middle point of a long piece of string underneath. For this method, there is nothing more annoying than running out of string halfway through, so we suggest five feet (150 cm).

Wrap the string around, but this time cross at the three-quarter mark rather than at halfway. Run the strings around the other side and do it again and again, crossing at the corners until you can finally tie it off. As you'll see from the picture, the ends are not held by the string, but this is robust – and it leaves a space for the address.

EXTRAORDINARY STORIES – PART FOUR

Douglas Bader

> 'Rules are for the obedience of fools and the guidance of wise men'

> — Douglas Bader

Douglas Robert Bader was born on 10 February 1910 in London. His father Frederick was a civil engineer and when Douglas was just a few months old, he and his wife Jesse went out to work in India. They considered the climate too harsh for a baby and Douglas did not join them until he was two. The Bader family came back to England in 1913, though with the outbreak of World War I, Frederick Bader went with the army to France. Douglas never saw his father again. He died there after complications with a shrapnel wound.

His mother Jesse remarried, but Douglas spent a great deal of time with his aunt Hazel Bader and her husband, Flight Lieutenant Cyril Burge, who was adjutant to the RAF college at Cranwell. Through that relationship, Bader discovered a love of planes and flying that would last him the rest of his life. He had been a superb sportsman at St Edward's school in Oxford and after becoming a cadet at Cranwell in 1928, he represented the college at boxing,

cricket, hockey and rugby. His academic studies were not as impressive and he came second for the sword of honour at graduation. One of the students said, 'To us, Bader was a sort of god who played every conceivable game and was the best player in every team'. He was commissioned as an RAF officer in 1930.

He was an extremely gifted pilot and gained a place in his squadron aerobatics team, winning the pairs title at the Hendon pageant of 1931. He was absolutely without fear and pushed his bi-plane a little too far on 14 December that year. He was showing off to friends with low rolls barely above the ground. One wingtip touched and the plane crashed, doing terrible damage to his legs. Dr Leonard Joyce had to amputate his right leg above the knee, his left below.

The twenty-one-year-old Bader was not expected to survive, but he had a fierce will to live and a furious temper. He began the slow painful path to recovery and was transferred to the RAF hospital at Uxbridge. He met the great love of his life, Thelma Edwards, there and married her in 1935.

Bader was given metal artificial legs and had to learn to use them, as well as grow callouses on his stumps. The right leg was particularly tricky as the metal knee joint required great balance and perseverance. He was told he should use the sticks to help his progress as he would never walk without them. Bader replied, 'On the contrary, I will never bloody walk with them.' He never did, relying instead on his reflexes, coordination and sheer will. His life had altered for ever. Later, Bader recorded the event in his flying log with these words:

'X-country Reading. Crashed slow rolling near ground. Bad show.'

After being discharged from the RAF, Bader went to work for the Asiatic Petroleum Company. As he couldn't fly, he drove a specially adapted sports car like a maniac along country lanes, but there was more to come in the life of this extraordinary man. When the Second World War broke out in 1939, Douglas immediately attempted to re-enlist. He was refused at first, being told that there was nothing in the King's regulations allowing a man in his condition to fly. He retorted that there was nothing in the King's regulations to say a man in his condition couldn't fly!

He had the support of his fellow officers, especially those who had known him from before the accident. Britain needed pilots and Bader was taken back into the RAF and made flight commander of 222 Squadron, flying and making his first kill as they covered the retreat at Dunkirk. He was promoted after that action to command the Canadian 242 Squadron. They had lost half their number in casualties and were severely demoralised. With his metal legs, they assumed at first that he would lead them from behind a desk, but instead, he demonstrated aerobatics to them for an hour, flying a Hurricane fighter. Douglas Bader was the right man to restore their morale through his peculiar brand of stubbornness and charismatic leadership. From the beginning, he trained them in his own style of fighting, ignoring the Fighter Command official tactics. In fact, his ideas would prove their usefulness and became effective tactics for the RAF in resisting the German bombers and fighter escorts.

Under Bader, 242 Squadron first fought in the Battle of Britain on 30 August 1940 against the German fighter waves, taking down twelve German planes in a single hour. They would go on to fly three or four sorties a day for as long as their Hurricanes would stand up to the punishment.

HAWKER "HURRICANE I"

Bader himself was responsible for 22½ air-to-air victories – the half after he and a friend shot up a German plane together and both agreed to claim half the kill. The total made him the fifth highest ace in the RAF. The importance of this cannot be overestimated. Without air superiority, Britain could not have defended her cities or airfields in WWII. German bombers would have had a free hand as they had over in Europe. Bader was awarded the Distinguished Flying Cross (DFC) and the Distinguished Service Order (DSO) for gallantry and leadership at the Battle of Britain.

In the lull after the battle, Bader continued to take his squadron out to attack German E-boats and the occasional lone Dornier bomber. He was a key player in the revision of RAF and US Air Force tactics, commanding the Tangmere wing of three squadrons as they prowled over the Channel looking for the enemy. When returning from successful missions, Bader was in the habit of opening his cockpit canopy and lighting a pipe with the control stick held between his metal knee and his good knee. When other pilots saw him do this, they kept a good distance in case he blew the plane up with petrol fumes.

In 1941, he was involved in a mid-air collision over France with a German Me 109 whilst dogfighting. The tail of Bader's plane was torn off and he was began plummeting towards the ground. He got the canopy off and climbed out into the wind to parachute clear. His right leg caught and he found himself nailed to the fuselage by the slipstream, heaving and tugging at the metal leg before it took him down with the plane. At last, the belt holding the leg to him snapped and the leg went off through his trousers, allowing him to break free of the plane and parachute to safety.

In German captivity, he asked if a message could be sent to England for his spare right leg to be sent over. It is an astonishing thing, but the Germans agreed to this and the RAF dropped it in a crate during a normal bombing run. The leg was slightly damaged in the landing, but the Germans repaired it and took it to Bader in the hospital where he was being held. He put in on and while no one was paying attention, walked casually out of the hospital, in an attempt to escape. They caught him, but he maintained this spirit of cheerful defiance in various POW camps, inspiring respect from those around him. All British prisoners understood that escape attempts meant that more guards would be used who might otherwise be killing allied forces. Even failed attempts had value. Eventually, the Germans sent Bader to the famous Colditz Castle, which was meant to be escape-proof.

More than three hundred attempts were made over five years and thirty-one people did in fact get completely clear. The inmates built a complete glider, walked out dressed as German soldiers and generally forced the Germans to use vast resources and manpower to keep them in. Airey Neave was the first Briton to escape the castle. He later went on to become an MP and was killed in an IRA car bomb in 1979.

Bader attempted escape so many times that the Germans took his legs away. A great outcry was raised over this and the Germans were shamed into returning them. Bader promptly escaped again and had to be brought back. He was still there when the Americans liberated Colditz in 1945 and he returned to England, where he was promoted to group captain. With the war over, he couldn't see a future for himself in a peacetime RAF and instead joined Shell Oil's aviation department, a job that came with its own plane.

Bader raised money and campaigned for disabled people, flying all over the world visiting veterans' hospitals. He inspired others by his example and his willpower.

One day in 1955, he went back to speak at his old school in Oxford. A fifteen-year-old pupil saw Group Captain Bader coming through the gates with his instantly recognisable gait. Bader was carrying cases and it was a hot day, so the boy ran across and offered to help with the bags. Bader's response was to tell him to 'bugger off!' in a very angry tone. The headmaster came to see the boy later. He said that he had done the right thing in offering, but 'Group Captain Bader will not be helped. He regards carrying his own cases on a blazing hot day as a challenge.'

The book and film 'Reach for the Sky' tell the man's story better than we have here. Bader was always a prickly, difficult personality, but his courage and stubbornness were legendary. He died in 1982, but his story is still an inspiration.

THE GAME OF CHESS

―――――✦―――――

CHESS IS AN ANCIENT board game that came to Europe along the silk route from China and India. It is a game of war and tactical advantage, played by generals and princes down through the ages. Its exact origins are unknown, though the pieces may be based on the ancient formations of Indian armies.

It is a game for two people, played on a board of sixty-four alternately black and white squares. As with most of the best games, it is easy to play badly and hard to play well.

THE PIECES

Both sides have sixteen pieces: 8 pawns, 2 knights, 2 bishops, 2 castles, (also known as rooks), 1 queen and 1 king.

The object of the game is to capture (checkmate) the opponent's king. White has the first move and then both players take it in turns until one triumphs.

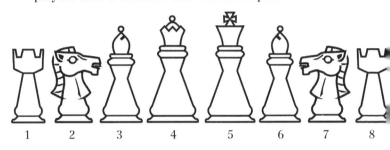

1   2   3   4   5   6   7   8

SETTING UP THE BOARD

There should be a white square in the right-hand corner when placing the board. The pieces are arranged in two lines, facing each other. The pawns protect the rear line, which is arranged in the following sequence: 1. Rook; 2. Knight; 3. Bishop; 4. Queen; 5. King; 6. Bishop; 7. Knight; 8 Rook.

The queen always goes on her own colour – the black queen on the black square in the middle. The white queen will go on the corresponding white square.

Movement and Values

Each type of piece moves in a different way.

1. **Pawns** are the infantry and move forward, one square at a time – except on the first move, where they are allowed to lurch two squares forward in a fit of martial enthusiasm. They capture diagonally, to the left or right. They are the least valuable pieces, but the only ones that can be promoted. (Value: 1 point.)

2. The **Knights** are the cavalry: mobile and difficult to stop. They move in an 'L' shape of 'two squares and one' in any direction. In the diagram, all the black pawns around the knight can be attacked. Crucially, the knight is the only

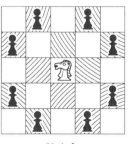

Knight

piece that can jump over others in their path. Even if a rook blocked the way to one of the pawns above, the knight could still take the pawn. (Value: 3 points.)

3. **Bishops** are the elephants. They move along the diagonals, though they are limited to white or black squares only. They work well together, covering both colour squares. They also do well in distance attacks, like machine guns or searchlights. (Value: 3 points.)

4. **Castles** (Rooks). These are the chariot forces. They control the straight lines on the board and are particularly useful in the endgame and for castling. (Value 5 points.)

5. The **Queen**. This is the most powerful piece on the board and can move in any direction, without limit. (Value 8 points.)

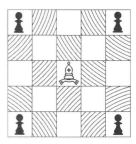

Bishop

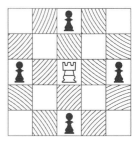

Rook/Castle

Queen

6. The **King** is the most important piece on the board. It can only move one square at a time, but in any direction. It can move two squares whilst castling. It cannot move into check. (Value: Game.)

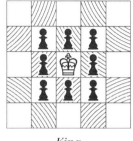

King

The Game

Having the first move is an advantage and most games tend to be won by white. Classically, black plays defensively, countering white's aggressive moves and taking advantage of mistakes.

Capturing. One player removes an enemy piece from the board by landing on the same square. With the exception of a king, any piece can take any other. A king is restricted by the fact that it cannot move into check, so a king can never take another king. Pawns can only capture diagonally, moving forward.

Check/Checkmate. If a piece threatens the king, so that in theory it could take the king, it is called 'check'. The king *must* either move out of check, block the check, or the attacking piece must be taken. If none of these are possible, the king has been caught – a checkmate, which is a corruption of the Arabic for 'The king is dead'.

Castling. After the knight and bishop have moved, the king can shift two squares either left or right, with the rook taking the inside square.

Castling Kingside

Castling Queenside

En Passant. This is an unusual form of pawn capture that is now common practice. When a pawn has moved down the board, it looks possible to avoid it by moving the opposing pawn two squares up. 'En passant' allows pawn capture as if only one square had been moved.

In theory, the game can be split into thirds – the opening, the middle game and the endgame.

OPENING

The idea here is to get out all your main pieces, known as
'developing', before castling your king to safety. The centre
of the board (the four central squares) is important to control. For example, a knight in the centre has up to eight
possible moves. In a corner, he may only have two.

Some openings have names and long histories, such as
'The King's Indian Defence' and 'The Sicilian'. There are
many books on openings, but you should find one you like
and stick to it, playing it often to understand it better. As an
example, we'll show the moves of the King's Indian.

Remember, pawns cannot go backwards, so move them carefully as you develop. Link them into pawn chains, one protecting the next. Try and avoid leaving a piece 'en prise', or undefended.

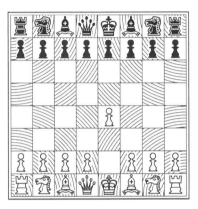

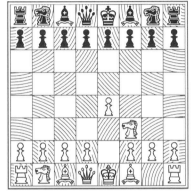

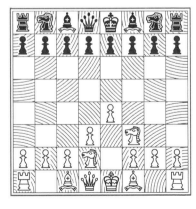

THE MIDDLE GAME

Your pieces should be developed and your king safe. This is where you start to attack.

Advance your pieces to positions that help control the board and capture the enemy units. Even at this stage, you should be looking for opportunities to capture the enemy king, but don't overextend your pieces. If you want to move to a square with one piece, make sure it is protected by another.

A 'pin' is a piece held in place by the danger of losing a more important piece behind it. Pins work particularly well against the enemy king. Your opponent is unable to move his blocking pieces as he *cannot* move into check.

A 'fork' is when a piece threatens two pieces at the same time. The knight is particularly good at this and can be deadly when putting the king in check and at the same time threatening a valuable piece.

A 'skewer' is the opposite of a pin, when a valuable piece is forced to move, thereby exposing a lesser piece to capture. A rook that threatens a queen may not get the queen, but may take the bishop behind her when she moves.

Remember to keep your king protected in your 'castle', stay level on points and try to get ahead. Even a pawn advantage will show itself in the endgame.

THE ENDGAME

It is possible to win in the middle game, while the board is still full of pieces, but most wins occur in the endgame. The board will be stripped of the main pieces and pawns. Strangely, the safest position for the king is now the centre of the board, where its power can be used to attack and shepherd pawns towards promotion.

Promotion. If a pawn reaches the back rank of the opposing side, it can be exchanged for a queen, rook, bishop or knight. (You can have two queens! Just turn a rook upside down to represent the second one.) In the endgame, the threat of promotion can have a serious effect on tactics.

The endgame will involve combinations of pieces, as bishops and rooks, for example, attempt to limit the enemy king's movement, check him and then bring about a checkmate. Rooks are particularly strong in the endgame and should not be sacrificed early.

The aim is obviously to checkmate your opponent's king. This is the hardest part of the game and the last thing the novice learns to do *well*.

This is one of the only games where you get to match your brain directly against someone else. It's a level playing field – except for experience, preparation and intelligence. Do not underestimate preparation. Many a clever boy has been beaten by a better chess player.

It is played all over the world, from magnetic sets on trains to ornate bone carved sets in Indonesia. It's a language we all know and every boy should be able to play chess.

THE SINGLE GREATEST RACE OF ALL TIME

THE MILLE MIGLIA 1955

The Mille Miglia (thousand mile) road race took place only twenty-four times before being banned. It was a race from Brescia in Italy, across the northern plain, down the Adriatic coast, across the mountains to Rome, then to Bologna and back up to Brescia. Although the route was closed to normal traffic, the cars drove on rough single-carriageway roads, along hair-pin bends and through the streets of towns with only a few straw bales to protect the crowds. The first race in 1927 was an all Italian affair and ended in just over twenty-one hours. It quickly became the ultimate road race and the one that all racing drivers wanted to win. Mussolini stopped it briefly in 1938 after a number of spectators were killed, but it resumed in 1940. The final race of 1957 ended with a crash that took the lives of Alfonso de Portago, his navigator and ten spectators.

On 1 May, 1955, the British racing driver Stirling Moss was in position at the start line. He had Denis 'Jenks' Jenkinson with him as navigator and they had mapped the route on a roll of paper that Jenks unrolled as they went. As well as developing a system of hand-signals for Jenks to warn Moss about an upcoming corner, they had graded

them as 'saucy ones', 'dodgy ones' or 'very dangerous ones'. As it was a timed race, Moss knew that he needed every edge he could get if he was to beat Juan Manuel Fangio, twice Formula One world champion and still considered by many to be the greatest driver of all time. In an identical car, Fangio chose to drive alone and would complete the run on roads he knew as well as any in the world.

The cars were numbered according to their start time, so that Moss drove 722 and began at 7.22 in the morning. His car, shown here, was a Mercedes Benz 300SLR, with a 3.0 litre, straight eight engine, drum brakes and no seatbelts or safety equipment. It was capable of a top speed of 170mph.

Exactly ten hours, seven minutes and forty eight seconds later, they returned. It was a new record for the course. The car was battered and covered in brake dust and dirt. With no protection from the elements, Moss and Jenks themselves were black with grime. In an extraordinary feat of endurance and nerve, they had averaged just under a hundred miles an hour for the entire route, with Moss driving every straight flat out at 170mph and taking thousands of corners at the absolute limit of the car. They beat Fangio on his home roads by an incredible thirty minutes. Fangio would go on to win the world championship three more times before he retired, but Stirling Moss left him for dust at the Mille Miglia.

For many years afterwards, British police would stop speeding drivers with the words 'Who do you think you are then, Stirling Moss?'

ROLE-PLAYING GAMES

＊

This is not a page telling you *how* to do something – you'll see why as you read. It's a short essay on role-playing games: what they are and how to get started. There are few inventions of the twentieth century that can combine entertainment with imagination so well.

Dungeons and Dragons was put together in 1972. It is still available from online bookshops or gamer stores. To get started you'll need the player's handbook, the dungeon master's handbook, some dice and, eventually, an adventure to play. It isn't that cheap to start, but after the initial outlay, costs are minimal – it's all imagination and the occasional pencil.

In essence, you buy the books, read them and choose a character for yourself. There are basic classes like Fighter, Thief and Magic-user. The character will start out with certain qualities such as dexterity and strength, decided by the roll of a die. With experience, the character grows in power, endurance and knowledge. The game also grows more and more complex. Fighters win more powerful weapons, Wizards gain access to greater spells. When we were children, we progressed from Basic to Advanced to Expert to Immortal levels, before moving on to battling at a national level and building an empire. You never forget the first time you are exiled from a country you raised from nothing.

You do need a few people for this – it is a social game, which is a recommendation. In a very real sense, it is a training ground for the imagination and, in particular, a school for plot and character. It may even be a training ground for tactics. If you want to be a writer, try D&D. For that matter, if you want to be a mathematician, try D&D.

The Dungeon Master (or DM) is the one who runs the game. He will either collect or write adventures – literally set in dungeons or just about anywhere. The characters battle the monsters he chooses and either solve his traps or fall prey to them, suffering horrible deaths. The players will develop characters with extraordinarily detailed histories, equipment and skills.

For us, D&D meant hundreds of hours at school and at home playing with pencils, charts, dice and laughter. If elves don't grab you, there are many other forms of role-playing – from Judge Dredd, to superheroes, to Warhammer, to a hundred more . . . but Dungeons and Dragons is still the original and the best.

EXTRAORDINARY STORIES – PART FIVE

———— ✦ ————

Robert the Bruce (1274–1329)

AFTER A LONG and successful reign, King Alexander III of Scotland died in 1286 after falling from his horse. He left no surviving children and only one four-year-old granddaughter, Margaret, the daughter of the Norwegian king. Rather than see the realm splinter into factions, the Scottish lords proclaimed her queen, despite her youth. The King of England, Edward I, intended to marry her to his son, himself a baby at this stage. Sadly, Margaret died at the age of eight before even making it back to Scotland.

There were then *thirteen* claimants to the Scottish throne. Edward I of England was asked to adjudicate between them and he came north with an army to do so. In the end he chose John Balliol, who had a direct line back to King David I of Scotland (1124–1153). Robert the Bruce was the next strongest contender for the throne. He had a near identical claim back to David I, but he seems to have been an extraordinarily charismatic leader and practical politician, which Balliol was not. Balliol had English estates and Edward assumed he would not resist the annexation of Scotland after his coronation. However, Balliol did just that. He refused to give judicial or feudal authority to Edward, or to acknowledge his superiority in any form. Edward's attempt to gain Scotland by stealth and subtlety had come to nothing.

To put this period in historical context, it should be remembered that the great eras of expansion were still centuries away. The Elizabethan period was from 1558–1603. England and Scotland would not have a joint throne until James I and the beginning of the seventeenth century. England in the fourteenth century was feudal and bleak. Though cathedrals and universities soared in

Robert the Bruce

her cities, every aspect of life was ruled by the land-owning class and the Church of Rome. At the secular head was Edward I, King of England, a hard man intent on unifying his realm. He had already conquered Wales, naming his son as Prince. (There is an old story that when the Welsh were unhappy at the thought of an English prince to rule them, Edward said he would give them a prince who spoke no word of English. They cheered this, but then he held up his baby son to them . . .)

Robert the Bruce saw the reigns of two very different English kings. The first was Edward I, a man who has on his tomb the words 'Hic Est Edwardus Primus Scottorum Malleus' – Here lies King Edward, the Hammer of the Scots. In his younger years, Edward travelled as far as Jerusalem and Tunisia on the Crusades. After returning home, he conquered Wales, borrowing money from English Jews to do it. His solution to the mounting interest on his debts was to have 300 heads of Jewish families executed and the rest exiled in 1290.

When Edward turned his gaze on Scotland, hard years came to that country. When Balliol resisted Edward's authority, he knew war would follow and prepared an army to invade the north of England. Edward had also expected his support against the age-old enemy, France, but Balliol actually made a pact with France against him.

In a cold rage, Edward drove north with his professional soldiers, smashing all resistance with extraordinary savagery. At Berwick, his army butchered many thousands of men, women and children, killing for two days. The Scots destroyed crops and livestock, starving his men while they launched attacks into Northumberland. The north bled in thousands of skirmishes and murders. Edward captured the 'Stone of Destiny' from Scone, on which all Scottish monarchs had been crowned, taking it back to Westminster. It was placed in 'King Edward's Chair' (named after Edward the Confessor) in Westminster Abbey. All British monarchs since that time are crowned whilst sitting on that chair, including Elizabeth II in 1953. The actual stone was given back to the Scottish people in 1996, though it will be returned for future coronations, as the thrones are linked in a 'united kingdom'.

Balliol was forced to abdicate at Kincardine Castle, only five months after he had gone to war with Edward. He spent three years in the Tower of London before he was allowed to go to estates in France. Edward chose Berwick as the place where he would receive a formal oath of homage from 2,000 Scottish nobles that year. Robert the Bruce was one of those who swore fealty in 1296.

The Scots rebelled again and years of conflict followed – a turbulent period for Scotland that produced, amongst others, William Wallace, a romantic rebel against the English king. His life inspired Walter Scott to write *'Exploits and Death of William Wallace, the Hero of Scotland'* and he was also the inspiration for the film *Braveheart* in 1995. Wallace and Robert the Bruce did not always see eye to eye. Robert the Bruce was a better diplomat and Wallace supported John Balliol's right to be king of Scotland, saying his abdication was achieved under duress. Wallace achieved some extraordinary victories against the English armies, even when heavily outnumbered, as at the Battle of Stirling Bridge in 1297. For that action, Wallace was knighted by Robert the Bruce and named 'Guardian of the kingdom of Scotland and leader of its armies'.

However, in 1298, Wallace saw his army broken at the Battle of Falkirk. Wallace resigned as Guardian and the post was then shared between Robert the Bruce and John Comyn, another of the original thirteen with a claim to the throne. Wallace escaped and spent time in France while Robert the Bruce made peace with Edward in 1302, staying at court in Carlisle. All the leading Scots were forced to swear fealty to Edward again in 1304 – except for Wallace. He remained at large for another year, a popular hero wherever rebels met. He was finally caught in 1305 and was hanged, drawn, quartered and beheaded at Smithfield Market in London along with his brother, their heads placed on London Bridge. It must have seemed like the end of Scottish independence, but Edward was growing old and sick and his son would never be the man to rule the hard lands of the north. Edward II lacked charisma and personal authority. He would be one of the worst kings England ever had.

Robert the Bruce met with John Comyn to put the case for one of them becoming king of Scotland and breaking faith with Edward I. Though Comyn agreed at first, he announced the treachery in letters to King Edward. Warned by a friend, Robert was forced to ride from Carlisle to Scotland before he could be caught and executed. He arranged a meeting with John Comyn in the sanctuary of a Scottish church and he and his men killed Comyn there, in revenge for the betrayal. Robert the Bruce was later excommunicated for this act by Pope Clement V.

He was crowned King of Scotland by his own mistress in 1306 at Scone – though not with the famous stone under his feet. His reign did not start well, with a string of defeats against the English forces in Scotland. Three of his brothers were killed by Edward, his wife was taken prisoner and he was forced into hiding. The legend is well known that when he was on the run and forced to take shelter in a cave, he saw a spider trying to complete a web and failing, over and over. As Robert the Bruce watched, it tried again and succeeded. The example gave him hope.

In 1307, Robert the Bruce began a new rebellion and Edward I took an army north to crush him. Edward was old and exhausted and as he reached the borders of England and Scotland, he was taken ill at a place called Burgh-by-Sands, where he could actually see Scotland across the Solway Firth. He told his son not to entomb him in Westminster, but instead to boil the flesh off his bones and then carry the bones in every future battle until the Scots were destroyed. His son failed in this, as he failed his father in almost every way. He faced problems of rebellious lords in England and returned there, leaving Robert the Bruce alone to consolidate his position.

In 1308, the tides of war changed for Robert the Bruce. He fought the Comyns first to establish his claim and then had the French king recognise his right to rule Scotland, which was a great aid to his cause. Considering that Edward II had married the French king's daughter Isabella, it was an astonishing feat of diplomacy. In fairness, the marriage could not have been a happy one. One of Edward

II's first orders as King was to bring his lover, Piers Gaveston, back from France, where his father had banished him.

Robert the Bruce was also aided by Sir James Douglas, known as 'The Black Douglas'. Under his command, the Scottish clan forces drove out the English garrisons Edward I had left and invaded the north of England twice in 1311, laying the land waste.

Edward II had no choice but to respond. He took a large army north against the forces under Bruce. An absolutely crucial battle followed – Bannockburn, still seen today as one of the classic dates in Scottish history. The Scottish forces were badly outnumbered and facing professional soldiers well armed with crossbow, longbow, sword, axe, pike and horse. The lie of the land played a part, as the English found themselves hemmed in by marsh ground and bog, negating their numerical superiority. The battle itself took place over two days, with the most serious clash on 24 June 1314. The English cavalry charge was ineffective on that ground and was beaten back. The Scottish advance rolled over the English archers and the victory was complete when Edward II fled the field, his nerve deserting him.

Robert the Bruce would go on to many other victories over the next decade. The Irish lords even offered him the throne of Ireland. Robert sent his brother Edward, who was crowned High King of Ireland in 1316.

In England, Edward II managed to sire two boys and two girls with Isabella, despite his inclinations. He lacked the ruthlessness and tactical skill of his father, and Robert the Bruce was laying waste to cities and towns and sacking monasteries as far south as York. Edward II lost power to a committee of his own lords, lost his throne to his wife and eldest son and, after being held prisoner and tortured, was eventually put to death in 1327 by being impaled on a length of red-hot iron, considered at the time to be a suitable comment on his lifestyle and failures.

It would be Edward II's son, Edward III, who would sign a peace treaty in 1328 that recognised Scotland as an independent nation and Robert the Bruce as King. It was the crowning moment of Robert's life and he died the following year in 1329.

As he signed the treaty, Edward III was only sixteen and under his mother's legal power. When he reached his majority, he repudiated the treaty. English kings continued to call themselves rulers of Scotland, but Scotland did remain independent until 1603, when James VI of Scotland became James I of England and joined the thrones. Unlike his hopeless father, Edward III ruled successfully and wisely for no less than fifty years.

Robert the Bruce's final instruction was that his heart be taken to the Holy Land. It has since been returned and is buried in Melrose Abbey in Roxburghshire in the east of Scotland.

BOOKS EVERY BOY SHOULD READ

THE DANGER HERE is that you'll try to read books that are too hard for your age. The choices are from those books we enjoyed, but this is a list that all *men* should have read when they were boys. The first ones are the easiest – though not the best. Every title has been loved by millions. Like a reference to Jack and the Beanstalk, you should know Huckleberry Finn, Sherlock Holmes and all the other characters who make up the world of imagination. The list comes with suggested reading ages – but these are only rough minimums. Reading ability is more important than age.

1. Roald Dahl's books. From five up, these can be read to children. *The Twits* is fantastic. *Charlie and the Chocolate Factory*, *George's Marvellous Medicine*, *The BFG*, and *James and the Giant Peach* are all worth reading. For older readers, his short stories are nothing short of brilliant.

2. The Winnie-the-Pooh books by A.A. Milne. Beautifully written, amusing stories.

3. Willard Price – a series of adventure books, with titles such as *Underwater Adventure*, *Arctic Adventure* and so on. The two main characters, Hal and Roger, are role models for all boys growing up today. Suitable for ages eight and above.

4. All the Famous Five books by Enid Blyton. Also, her Secret Seven series. These are classic adventure and crime stories for those aged eight and above, up to the early teens.

5. *Fungus the Bogeyman* by Raymond Briggs. One of the strangest books in this list, but oddly compelling. For all ages, but probably ten and above.

6. *Grimm's Fairy Tales*; Hans Christian Andersen; Greek and Roman legends. There are many collections out there, but these stories have survived because they are good.

7. *The Belgariad* by David Eddings. Fantasy series of five books, every one a gem. Eleven and above.

8. *Rogue Male* by Geoffrey Household. An extraordinary story of survival against the odds. Suitable for eleven and over.

9. *The Lion, the Witch and the Wardrobe* by C.S. Lewis. The second of the Narnia series. Superb fantasy stories for confident readers of twelve and above.

10. *Charlotte's Web*, by E.B. White. A powerful story of a pig and a spider! Eight years old and up.

11. *Kim* by Rudyard Kipling – a classic adventure. Also, the *Just So Stories* and *The Jungle Book*. For confident readers, but well worth the time.

12. *The Thirty-Nine Steps* by John Buchan. This is almost the definition of a boy's adventure story, involving spies and wild dashes across the Scottish countryside. Also look for *Mr Standfast* by the same author.

13. The James Bond books by Ian Fleming. For early teen readers and above. These stories are quite dark in places – far grittier than the films.

14. The Harry Potter books by J.K. Rowling. Modern classics.

15. *1066 and All That* by W.C. Sellar and R.J. Yeatman. A funny book of British history, packed with interesting information, though how much it will help with real history is anyone's guess. Early teens and above.

16. Mark Twain – *The Adventures of Tom Sawyer* and *The Adventures of Huckleberry Finn*. For confident readers of twelve and above

17. Isaac Asimov – science fiction. He wrote hundreds of

brilliant short stories, available in collections. Confident readers of twelve and above.

18. Terry Pratchett's Discworld books. They are all fantastic, funny and interesting. Start with *Sourcery*. Twelve and above.

19. *Ender's Game* by Orson Scott Card. Fantastic story of a young boy in a military academy. Confident readers of twelve and above.

20. *Midshipman's Hope* by David Feintuch. A space fantasy with a marvellous main character. There are seven in the full series.

21. *The Hitchhiker's Guide to the Galaxy* by Douglas Adams. Funny and clever – the old 'five books to a trilogy' ploy. Twelve and up.

22. David Gemmell's books, such as *Waylander* – the master of heroic fantasy for fourteen and up. Read one and you'll read them all.

23. *Magician* by Raymond E. Feist. One of the best fantasy novels ever written – and a whole series of first-class sequels to follow.

24. *The Lord of the Rings* by J.R.R. Tolkien. The masterwork trilogy. For confident teen readers.

25. Bernard Cornwell's Sharpe series. A terrific series of books, packed full of action and adventure. For confident readers of thirteen and above.

26. The Flashman books by George MacDonald Fraser. For confident readers, but a great dip into history and adventure. Fourteen and above.

27. *Animal Farm* and *1984* by George Orwell. Novels to wake the brain. For confident readers of fourteen and over.

28. *Brave New World* by Aldous Huxley. Like Orwell's *1984*, a famous story of a future we should fear.

29. *Lord of the Flies* by William Golding. Superb – but only for accomplished readers of fourteen and above.

30. H.G. Wells's *The Time Machine*, *The Island of Dr Moreau*, *The Invisible Man* – books from one of the best literary minds of the nineteenth century. Fourteen and above.

31. The Sherlock Holmes adventures by Arthur Conan Doyle. The original classic detective mysteries. Loads of short crime stories and longer novels, like *The Hound of the Baskervilles*. Accomplished readers only. Fifteen and above.

32. *Gulliver's Travels* by Jonathan Swift. One that can be read on more than one level. It gave us the lands of Lilliput and Brobdingnag.

33. *Three Men in a Boat* by Jerome K. Jerome. The funniest book ever written, but only for accomplished readers of fourteen or fifteen and above.

34. Stephen King. *The Bachman Books* is a good starting point. His novels are quite adult in subject and can be very frightening. Accomplished readers only – fifteen and above.

ILLUSTRATIONS

DANGEROUS THINGS
I HAVE LEARNT

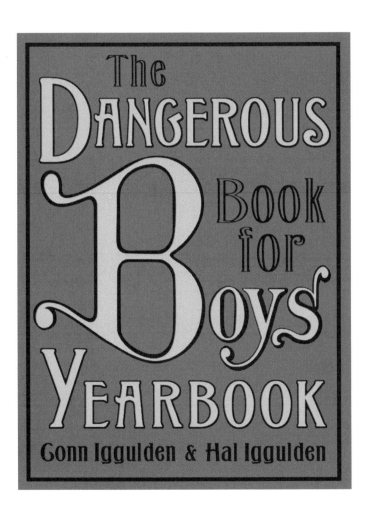

The
DANGEROUS
BOOK
for
Boys
YEARBOOK

Conn Iggulden & Hal Iggulden

THE DANGEROUS BOOK
FOR BOYS YEARBOOK

An event for every day
A story for every month
A flavour for every season
A book for you to make your own

Stuffed with seasonal activities to do with your friends: when is conker season? Where can I roll giant cheeses and why? What is flounder tramping and do I really want to do it?

Packed with useful historical facts to impress your friends: on what day was Isambard Kingdom Brunel born? When was the land speed record last broken and by whom? When were the Crown Jewels nearly stolen and how?

And, on top of Conn and Hal Iggulden's fascinating and fun facts, there is space for you to add your own notes and make this book your own. A book to treasure – and to use again and again.

ISBN 978 0 00 725539 9

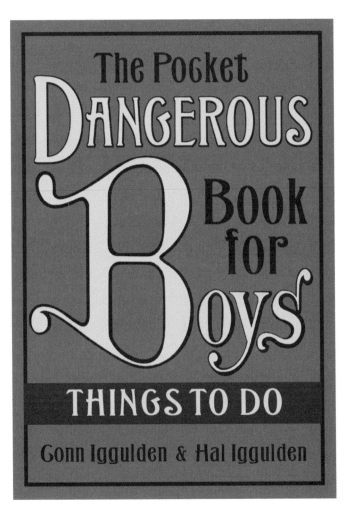

THE POCKET DANGEROUS
BOOK FOR BOYS: THINGS TO DO

The Dangerous Book for Boys inspired a newfound passion for adventure, fun and all things 'dangerous'. Now you have read *The Pocket Dangerous Book for Boys: Things to Know*, have you tried its companion book, the No. 1 bestseller *The Pocket Dangerous Book for Boys: Things to Do?*

With everything from how to win at poker, how to make a paper hat and how to skim stones to how to tie a knot and how to write a note in secret ink, *The Pocket Dangerous Book for Boys: Things to Do* is packed with fun things to do for every boy.

ISBN 978 0 00 725401 9

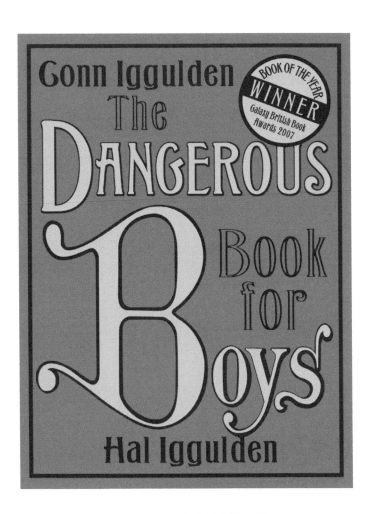

Conn Iggulden

The
DANGEROUS

BOOK
for
Boys

Hal Iggulden

BOOK OF THE YEAR
WINNER
Galaxy British Book
Awards 2007